I love Craig Etheredge's material! He believes in making disciples of everyone but then also specifically reveals how to disciple leaders. More than his ideas, I love that he is a practitioner of personal and organizational disciple making. If the church is to become what God desires, then men like Craig will have to show them how to do both as the art has been lost on most pastors in America.

Jim Putman, senior pastor of Real Life Ministries; author of *Real-Life Discipleship*

For a book on disciple making to be worthwhile for me, it must address a thorny issue I have been unable to solve. Early in his fine book, Craig Etheredge poses a question that grabbed my attention: How can we move people along a discipleship pathway while bringing them through a leadership pipeline to sustain a disciple-making movement? From then on, I found myself riveted. You won't be disappointed by his answer. I will be mining the wisdom contained in Craig's lived experience for the rest of my ministry.

Greg Ogden, Global Discipleship Initiative; author of *Discipleship Essentials*

I heartily recommend this important book to the growing library of disciple-making books by effective thinkers and practitioners. Craig has effectively lived out the principles of this book and helped many other leaders to follow his example. His life makes this book both profound and easy to apply.

Bobby Harrington, CEO of the National Disciple Making Forum, Discipleship.org, and Renew.org

The Disciple-Making Leader is a beautiful combination of a clear understanding of Christ's ministry, coupled with a practical grasp of the disciple-making pathway and the leadership pipeline! All are critically needed to develop movements of multiplying disciples. This book should be carefully read and discussed by all your leaders. The results will sharpen and strengthen your effectiveness in developing your leadership pipeline and multiplying disciples. Thank you, Craig, for a great work that will bear "much fruit" (John 15:8)!

Dann Spader, founder of Sonlife and Concentric Global; author of *4 Chair Discipling*, *Walk Like Jesus*, and *Live Like Jesus*

Disciple making is clearly the mission Christ gave His church; the problem is finding disciple- making leaders to lead the church. In *The Disciple-Making Leader*, Craig Etheredge gives very practical and helpful insight into how to develop disciple-making leaders in the church. With Christ as our example, Craig shares biblical principles for how to develop leadership out of discipleship. The combination of biblical principles from the life of Christ and years of pastoral experience makes this book a resource every pastor and church needs for developing church leaders who are disciple-making leaders. You will find *The Disciple-Making Leader* to be a handbook for leadership development that is timeless, transcendent, and transferrable.

Ken Adams, lead pastor of Crossroads Church; founder of Impact Ministries

How do we make more leaders? This is a frequent question posed by pastors and staff members. Jesus did not commission us to make leaders but to make disciples who will make disciples. But from these disciple makers, God calls leaders and leaders of leaders. The Great Commission precludes the leadership question and builds the church the way Jesus wants it. In this book, Craig Etheredge expertly examines and applies Jesus' model to help us become disciple-making leaders of disciple-making churches.

Daniel Edmonds, state missionary, Alabama Baptist State Board of Missions

CRAIG ETHEREDGE

THE DISCIPLE MAKING LEADER

Discover Jesus' Strategy for Raising up Leaders, Growing the Church, and Multiplying a Movement

Requests for information should be sent via e-mail to discipleFIRST.com. Visit discipleFIRST.com for contact information.

ISBN # 978-0-9993439-7-5 (Paperback)
ISBN # 978-0-9993439-8-2 (Kindle)
ISBN # 978-0-9993439-9-9 (ePub)

Cove and interior design: Harrington Interactive Media (harringtoninteractive.com)

DEDICATION

I could not have done this project without thanking those who have invested in my life. First and foremost, I must thank my precious wife, Liz, who has cheered me on and been my partner in making disciples for over thirty-five years. Also, I must thank Dann Spader, who taught me to love Jesus and to study Jesus' life as the model for life and ministry. Finally, I am indebted to First Colleyville, the church I love and have had the privilege of pastoring for fifteen years. They are a constant source of encouragement to me, and I see God using them to make a lasting difference in the world.

CONTENTS

INTRODUCTION

Building a team is hard work. No matter how well a person interviews, you never really know whom you have until you've hired them. Usually within eighteen months or so, you begin to realize the kind of person you've hired. Over the years, I've added some incredible leaders to the team who grew the ministry and walked before our people as a godly example. And I've brought people on the team who caused more harm than good. Both types looked promising in the beginning but turned out to be quite different. I'm now convinced the best way to raise up leaders is to grow them up from within. It stands to reason that if you can raise up a leader who has already been a part of your organization, they will most likely know what they are getting into and so will you.

This is of course what the early church did. All these leaders emerged from within the church, rising to various levels of leadership as they showed themselves to be people of character, filled with the Spirit and capable for the role. The apostles laid hands on them and installed them publicly as leaders in the church (Acts 6:6). However, today that practice has seemingly gone by the wayside, replaced by online search engines, headhunters, and job posts. Yet the questions remain: How do we find the right kind of leaders? What is the optimal kind of leader for ministry?

These questions led me to think more deeply about how we find, cultivate, and raise up leaders within our church. And in this process, I've discovered one kind of leader who multiplies the ministry and accelerates growth more than any other: the disciple-making leader.

In the chapters that follow, I will be making a case for what makes a disciple-making leader so special. In doing so, I'll put forward a definition of a disciple-making leader, reveal the internal DNA of this kind of leader that enables them to multiply leaders and grow the ministry, and also contrast the disciple-making leader with the far more common kind of leader we see today who promises results but never produces lasting growth.

Over the past twenty years, I've studied Jesus and how he developed leaders. I've learned that Jesus was not only a master disciple maker but also a master movement builder. Disciple making and movement building go hand in hand. The people who create movements of multiplication are those who know how to be disciples of Jesus and raise up disciples of Jesus.

JESUS WAS NOT ONLY A MASTER DISCIPLE MAKER BUT ALSO A MASTER MOVEMENT BUILDER.

I've also discovered the vital training components Jesus used to turn his followers into exponential multipliers. In fact, you can use the same elements of Jesus' training, which was a four-step pathway for growing multiplying disciples, to build multiplying leaders in your own ministry. I will also show you a simple five-level leadership pipeline model you can adapt to your own ministry context. However, the synergy of the pathway and the pipeline will reveal how you can make and multiply disciple-making leadership at every level of your ministry. In addition, I will add some practical leadership insights to help you build a culture of disciple making throughout your organization.

History matters. And what I am presenting in these pages is nothing new; rather, it is quite ancient. These principles have been proven repeatedly in different times and cultures. That is why along the way you will read several brief vignettes describing how God has used disciple-making leaders throughout church history to expand his kingdom and multiply disciples. I hope these stories will inspire you to make multiplying disciple-making leaders as we charge into the future.

Jesus once said, "The Kingdom of Heaven is like the yeast a woman used in making bread. Even though she put only a little yeast in three measures of flour, it permeated every part of the dough" (Matt. 13:33, NLT). The future movements of tomorrow rely on disciple-making leaders. The exponential growth of the church will not come via charismatic leaders who move the masses by their personalities but rather through godly men and women who work quietly and faithfully (like yeast through dough), investing in a few, making disciples, and multiplying leaders into an army that cannot be stopped.

PART 1

MAKING THE DISCIPLE-MAKING LEADER

1

THE POTENTIAL

Every leader has potential, but not every leader reaches their potential. Let those words sink into your mind for just a minute. Look at them one more time. *Every leader has potential, but not every leader reaches their potential.* Right now, you can probably think of someone you know who has tremendous potential but for some reason hasn't lived up to that potential. For some reason they have sold themselves short. They have failed to reach their own expectations.

We see this all the time in sports. A great athlete has all the talent in the world. All the coaches and pundits predict a meteoric rise to fame and stardom. They compare him to legends of the game and talk about how he could be the greatest of all time. But for some reason, that athlete never quite makes it. So much potential, so much promise, so few results.

Leaders are the same way. Some leaders have incredible talent, skill, vision, and instincts, but they only accomplish a small portion of what they *could* accomplish. The failure of leaders to reach their potential harms not only the leaders themselves but also the people they lead. Think about a failed leader. Think about what they could have accomplished. Think of how their organization could have thrived under their leadership. Think of the people influenced by that leader who could have been inspired to follow in their steps, but now they are left with disappointment and disillusionment. When a leader fails, organizations fail, and people fail.

I have seen this personally. Early in my ministry, I saw capable, talented, charismatic leaders full of vision and skill wash out and leave a trail of confusion and pain behind them. No doubt you've seen it too.

DERAILING

On December 18, 2017, excited passengers loaded the string of cars on the inaugural launch of a new high-speed passenger train along the Point Defiance Bypass that runs between Seattle and Portland. The Amtrak *Cascades* passenger train 501 departed Seattle that morning at 6:00 a.m. and quickly climbed to a speed of over eighty miles per hour. As it approached the bridge that spans Interstate 5, the lead locomotive with its twelve cars came off the tracks as it attempted to bank a left turn, sending passenger cars down an embankment, and careening onto the highway, crushing several vehicles along the road. When the dust settled, three people had lost their lives, and sixty-five others had serious injuries. Chris Karnes, a software developer who was on the train that morning, said, "It sounded like being on the inside of an aluminum can being crushed."[1]

Upon investigation, inspectors confirmed that the train had been traveling at 78 miles per hour in a 30-mile-per-hour zone at the time of the derailment. Sources later confirmed that the launch of the new high-speed train came before the installation of a Positive Train Control system (PTC) that automatically regulates a train's speed to prevent high-speed accidents. If the PTC had been engaged, this tragedy would have never happened.[2]

Over the years, I've seen many leaders derail. It's sad, but true. So many come out of the station with high hopes but crash somewhere along the way. Derailment is a tragedy and can have many causes. Some leaders derail because they are just not very coachable. You give them some advice, and they hear it but don't listen. They think they are the smartest in the room. Some just make bad choices. Those poor choices may be personal or professional, but for whatever reason, the choices keep them from moving forward. I've heard it said, "You make your choices, and then your choices make you." That is so true.

Some leaders derail because they run out of steam spiritually. They had a vibrant walk with God that was powerful and exciting, but over time their flame turned to a flicker and their passion for God grew cold. Ministry became a job to do rather than a calling to fulfill. You will never go the distance in ministry with your spiritual tank on empty.

Some leaders fail because they listen to the wrong voices. Some of those voices say, "You are not good enough. God will never use you," and the leaders fall into despair. Others hear voices that say, "You are the best ever, and no one is as good as you," and they fall into pride. Both voices lead to a dead end.

Some leaders struggle because they lead out of insecurity. They are so concerned with being known and recognized as successful that they make decisions based on their own self-interests and not the interests of others. But nothing is more dangerous to any organization than an insecure leader.

Leaders also fail for many other reasons: arrogance, anger, disappointment, immorality, distractions, hurts of the past—any one of these could keep you from reaching your full redemptive potential and send your ministry off the rails. In fact, by this point in your ministry you have probably had to battle several of these dangers. I know I have.

But one danger is less obvious but more dangerous than any of these. You won't hear about this danger on the news or from podiums as leaders read their resignation letters. This one danger is so secret, so concealed, that most will never know they have succumbed to its toxic influence until their ministries are long over. This danger is so deadly because from the outside it looks like success. It looks like winning. It hits every growth metric and is championed by most large ministry leaders, yet it robs you of the one thing that allows you to maximize your full redemptive potential.

What is this danger? The superstar syndrome.

SUPERSTAR SYNDROME

Incredibly successful people all have the superstar syndrome. They are the superstar. By their own determination, intelligence, and force of will, they excel in their field. Steven Spielberg, Oprah Winfrey, Tom Brady, Michael Jordan, Beyoncé, Jeff Bezos, Satoshi Nakamoto, and the list goes on and on. All these individuals became superstars because they performed at a level few can replicate. They are the superstar. They are the brand. Take them out of the equation, and everything collapses. And for many ministry leaders, this same concept of success permeates their thinking. They think successful ministry leaders are those who have the talent, the creativity, the charisma, and the skills necessary to build big ministries. This is what business guru Jim Collins calls "the genius with a thousand helpers."[3]

WHAT IS THIS DANGER? THE SUPERSTAR SYNDROME.

There is the superstar speaker, the superstar leader or visionary, and then there is everyone else. This is what I call the "superstar syndrome," and it's lethal. As superstar pastors and megachurch leaders who exemplify success in religious circles come to mind, you might think, *What's wrong with being great?* These are the people who speak at conferences, write books to explain how they made it to the top, and find positions on boards of powerful institutions. But is it possible to reach superstar status and not fully reach your redemptive potential? Also, can someone have a limitless impact that continues for generations and *not* be a superstar? The answer to both is yes. I'm merely making the point that chasing superstar status is bad for you. It can derail your ministry.

THE DARK SIDE OF STARDOM

Chasing superstar status is bad for two obvious reasons. First, few ever make it. It's like the lottery. Sure, someone is going to win the $50 million jackpot, but most won't. It's like becoming a sports professional. While over half of high school athletes believe they can play at the college level, only 1 out of 100 players make it onto a Division I team. And the odds of making it to the pros are even more daunting. Only 1 in 16,000 high school athletes will play professionally.[4]

The same is true of ministry leaders chasing stardom. Just from a statistical perspective, only a few will lead at the megachurch level. According to the National Congregational Study Survey, approximately 380,000 churches are in America.[5] However, only an estimated 1,750 qualify as "megachurches" (churches with more than 2,000 in weekly attendance). This means .004 percent of all churches are megachurches. So if superstar status (as defined by leading large ministries) is the sign of success, then success eludes the vast majority of those in ministry today.[6]

This is incredibly discouraging for most ministry leaders. Quite frankly, most pastors are tired. They have worked hard to move their ministries forward, and they see the reality dawning that they are probably not going to move their congregations into mega status. Does that mean they will never reach their full redemptive potential? That they have failed, or their ministry can't have an incredible impact? Of course not. But the allure of superstar status often whispers in their ears. The self-doubt lingers that what they are doing is good but not *as good* as others.

The other obvious problem with chasing superstardom is that for the few who do achieve it, stardom often becomes toxic to their personal spiritual health as well as the health of their ministries. A long list could be compiled of high-profile ministry leaders who had to step down for various reasons over the past decade. Each of them derailed, which is tremendously sad. The ripple effects of their sin hurt so many and leave them to wonder if those who profess Christ on the largest platforms are genuinely devoted followers of Jesus or just charlatans greedy for glory and gain. When leaders fall at this level, their congregations are left to pick up the pieces, some of which never recover. I talked recently with one couple who had just left the ministry of a fallen leader. They said, "It was so good, and then everything just fell apart." And the leader often fades into obscurity, never to return.

Chasing stardom isn't only alluring to lead pastors. I see associate pastors, worship pastors, and youth pastors often seeking stardom in their own respective fields. Mostly, these leaders possess the notion that they are the star, they are the real reason the ministry works. Their abilities cause the ministry to grow, and no one can do it like they can. And this mentality often leads to disappointment and heartbreak.

Pride lurks in every shadow when you chase stardom. As Peter writes, "Your enemy the devil prowls around like a roaring lion looking for someone to devour" (1 Pet. 5:8, NIV). The belief that you did this, you built this, and it's all about you is corrosive to the soul and leads down a destructive path.

Superstar status is also so devastating because it prevents you from doing the very things that unlock your redemptive potential and limitless impact. Superstar status requires you to be center stage. You are the genius with the thousand followers. You must leverage your skills and talents to draw the most to you. You are the superstar to carry the entire team on your shoulders. But unfortunately, the ministry will only be as good as the superstar. The ministry can only grow as large as the capacity of the superstar.

Further, while the superstar may be the force who causes the ministry to move forward, they can also become the lid that prevents the ministry from going further. Building a ministry on a superstar is incredibly limiting. And what about replacing the superstar once they're gone? Many ministries built on the personality of the superstar struggle to find anyone similar to move the ministry forward. Most never do and suffer decline.

But what if there is a better way?

Ministries that move beyond limits are ministries that continually find a way to raise up emerging leaders and empower them to lead.

Instead of the ministry built with one key leader at the top of the pyramid and a thousand "helpers" below, the alternative model flips the pyramid upside down and sees the key leader at the bottom, multiplying and empowering new, vibrant, innovative leaders who will grow the ministry beyond the leader's natural abilities.

This process creates the disciple-making leader.

THE DISCIPLE-MAKING LEADER

A growing interest in discipleship has sparked in recent years. National conferences, books, and resources have shone the spotlight on the glaring need of the American church for discipleship. While a few churches are growing via conversion growth, most ministries are in decline. Add to that the fact that cultural winds are turning against the church. Christians today are often seen as people who stand in the way of progressivism and societal change. Those who hold to biblical views on sexuality, family, humanity's being created in the image of God, the unity of the church, the exclusivity of salvation through Christ, the sinfulness of all people, the need for repentance and faith in Christ alone, and other core doctrinal positions are viewed as backward and on the wrong side of history.

How will churches navigate these divisive days? How will they produce true disciples who are equipped not only to survive but also thrive as they infiltrate our culture with the gospel? And how will the church continue to be nimble, flexible, and malleable to raise up leaders and multiply in the current environment? The secret is really no secret. We must raise up more disciple-making leaders.

This is a good place to stop and provide a definition:

> A disciple-making leader leads out of the overflow of their walk with Christ and intentionally invests in others to produce genuine disciples and ministry leaders who will multiply the movement.

Now let me break this definition down into its three important parts.

1. *Personal Walk with Christ.* The disciple-making leader leads out of the overflow of their personal walk with Jesus Christ. Most important to the disciple-making leader is, first and foremost, the authenticity of their devotion to Christ.

Now you may think this is true of any Christian leader, but that would be false. Many people find themselves in positions of leadership simply because they have mastered skills for the job, not because they have a genuine devotion to Jesus. If the student pastor is energetic, if the worship pastor is talented, if the children's pastor is creative, if the executive pastor is a good manager, or if the lead pastor is a dynamic communicator, then they can rise to positions of leadership. A healthy devotion to Jesus is assumed. Unfortunately, the demands of the job often suffocate what intimacy they once had with Christ. So a genuine walk with God is where leadership begins.

2. *Intentional Investment in Others.* The disciple-making leader intentionally invests their life in others. Their goal is to reproduce themselves in the lives of others. They constantly recruit, select, train, invest in, and appoint new leaders. They fill their leadership teams with people who think like them, act like them, and do ministry like them. Instead of being the only genius with a thousand helpers, they want to raise up a thousand leaders to expand the ministry far beyond their ability.

This investment takes place in two areas—both spiritually and professionally. The disciple-making leader begins with spiritual investment. They spend time helping those under their care to understand how to know and follow Jesus in a deep and personal way. The disciple-making leader trains them to walk with God, to reach their world, and to invest in a few. But the investment doesn't stop there. The disciple-making leader also invests in others professionally, taking what they have learned and instilling it in those under them so they master the same skills.

Why do they do this? This leads to the last part of our definition.

3. *Leadership Multiplication.* The end goal of the disciple-making leader is multiplication. The goal is to raise up more disciple-making

leaders like themselves so the ministry will multiply into an unstoppable movement. Think about the early church. Only 120 believers were in the upper room waiting for the Spirit's coming, but those few multiplied greatly and quickly spread over the known world. Without multiplication there is no movement. But when leaders multiply themselves into other leaders who do the same, the kingdom of God benefits. One hundred years from now, probably no one will remember the disciple-making leader's name, but their impact and investment will still bear fruit. That explains more fully the definition of a disciple-making leader.

THE DISCIPLE-MAKING LEADER IS FOCUSED ON RAISING UP OTHERS.

Do you see now the difference between the superstar and the disciple-making leader? The superstar is focused on "me," but the disciple-making leader is focused on raising up others. Talent and ambition fuel the superstar; on the other hand, a personal walk with Christ and God's calling on their life fuels the disciple-making leader.

Superstar	**Disciple-Making Leader**
Longs to be known.	Longs to be faithful.
Relationships are not as important as results.	Ministry is relational.
Finds joy in his accomplishments.	Finds joy in the accomplishments of those they lead.
Wants others to serve them.	Wants to serve others.
Impact dies with them.	Impact lives long after they are gone.

THE ULTIMATE DISCIPLE-MAKING LEADER

The year was 1943. A Jesuit priest named Tomislav Poglajen fled his home country of Croatia and settled in Czechoslovakia. To avoid detection by the Nazi Gestapo, he changed his last name to his mother's maiden name, Kolakovic, and he took up a teaching post in the city of Bratislava.

He was only thirty-seven years old, but he possessed a keen insight into the winds of the culture. He knew that when the Nazis were defeated, the Soviets would take over Czechoslovakia, and he wanted to prepare his students. He knew persecution would come, which would put believers to the greatest test. In preparation, he gathered his students in his home. There they read the Bible and prayed together. He taught them to commit their lives to Christ completely. Only this would enable them to stand under the coming trials. By the end of 1944, disciples of Kolakovic had multiplied to almost every campus in their city and to surrounding cities. He taught them a three-word motto: "See. Judge. Act." See what is happening around you. Judge them according to what you know is biblically true. Act to resist evil and stand courageously.[7]

After Czechoslovakia fell to the Soviets, Father Kolakovic was expelled from the country, and many of his students were arrested, just as he had predicted. But after Kolakovic's students emerged from prison in the 1960s, they began doing what they had been taught. They gathered in homes. They studied God's Word. They devoted their lives to Jesus. They prayed. They acted wisely. They spoke with courage and boldness. And they built the underground church, which became the nucleus of the resistance movement, resulting in the fall of communism in that country.

Kolakovic was not a superstar by any stretch. He worked in the shadows, undetected. He didn't draw crowds. He didn't seek the spotlight or leverage people in powerful positions. Instead, he invested in a few students at a time and taught them to think like him, act like him, and multiply like him. He wasn't a superstar leader; he was a disciple-making leader. And although you probably have never heard the name Tomislov Kolakovic before, you have seen his influence. The freedom of Czechoslovakia is the result of his life and work.

In a much greater way, Jesus was the ultimate disciple-making leader. Jesus didn't choose the superstar status, even though if anyone could have done it, it would have been Jesus. After all, he was God in the flesh. The apostle John makes this clear:

> In the beginning was the Word, and the Word was with God, and the Word was God. He was with God in the beginning. All things were created through him, and apart from him not one thing was created that has been created. In him was life, and that life was the light of men. . . . The Word became flesh and dwelt among us. We observed his glory, the glory as the one and only Son from the Father, full of grace and truth. (John 1:1–5, 14)

But Jesus chose the alternative strategy. He chose to be a disciple-making leader. Instead of exalting himself, he humbled himself and took on the form of a servant (Phil. 2:5–11). Instead of focusing his ministry strategy on his ability to draw crowds, he focused his primary attention on selecting, calling, training, and investing in a few men. According to Dann Spader's biblical research, Jesus spent seventeen occasions with the crowds, ministering to the masses, but he spent forty-six occasions with the few men he trained for ministry impact. His priority was clear.

Someone once said Jesus didn't come to change the world but came to change twelve men who would change the world. He spent a little over three and a half years training these men to think and act like him. He said, "A disciple is not above his teacher, but everyone who is fully trained will be like his teacher" (Luke 6:40). And after Jesus was gone, his followers, filled with the Holy Spirit, continued his ministry in his name. Though they were "unschooled, ordinary men," they clearly had been with Jesus (Acts 4:13, NIV). They went on to fill Jerusalem with their teachings (Acts 5:28) and turn the world upside down (Acts 17:6).

And the evidence of Jesus' life and work is the men and women around the world who have responded to the gospel.

Jesus never wrote a book, never went to college, never held office, never traveled worldwide, and never led a major company. He was born into poverty, lived in obscurity, worked with his hands, traveled by foot, and made his bed under the stars. Many loved him, some hated him, and most ignored him. He died as a criminal, was buried as a pauper, and was thought to have accomplished nothing.

Yet no one has ever left an impact on the world like Jesus. His influence can be felt throughout history. His followers have shaped every aspect of culture from education and literature to science, government, and the arts. The churches founded in his name penetrate every known language, culture, and people group on the planet.

How do you explain this impact? He didn't acquire this influence through positions of power or accommodating people of means. He simply invested his life in a few men, who invested their lives in a few, who then invested their lives in a few. And the movement of multiplication that these men started still expands around the globe today. And what Jesus began, he calls you to continue until he comes again.

WHAT JESUS BEGAN, HE CALLS YOU TO CONTINUE.

THE SCARCITY OF LEADERS

We are in desperate need of disciple-making leaders in the church today. In my experience, these are rare finds. Instead, two types of leaders exist in most churches today; those who have never been discipled and those who have been discipled but never reach their leadership potential. The first type are capable men and women who sense a call to ministry, some have even spent years in seminary training and have come up through the ranks of church leadership, but they have never been personally discipled.

This was my own story. I grew up in church. My father was a full-time worship pastor so all I've ever known is being in church. In fact,

I like to say I was in the alto section of the church choir nine months before I was born. At age seven, I distinctly recall hearing the gospel preached on a Sunday morning. My heart raced. My attention was fixed on every word. After the service I met with one of our pastors and asked Jesus to forgive me and lead my life. It was in every way a life-altering moment. After that initial conversion, most of my discipleship training came through church programs and conversations at home.

When I was in college, a young couple took me and my girlfriend (who became my wife, Liz) under their wing and began teaching us how to study the Bible. It was a tremendous time of growth for me. A few years later, God clearly called me to vocational ministry. I spent four years in seminary training for the ministry. During that time, I worked in various roles on one church's staff, spending time as a youth intern, interim youth pastor, college pastor, young adult pastor—you name it, I did it. I rose up through the leadership ranks, and with every step my ministry responsibilities grew. I also received opportunities to preach and lead at the highest levels. Yet not until I was the senior pastor of a church did I meet men who knew how to make disciples.

I watched three businessmen in our church regularly share their faith, following up with new believers and multiplying disciple makers. And I realized in that moment that while I loved the Lord and was called to ministry, I didn't know how to make disciples. While I was proficient as a leader, I was woefully deficient as a disciple maker. I thought the sign of successful ministry was numerical growth under my leadership. It never occurred to me that successful ministry was not just measured by the number in my ministry but by the number of disciple-making leaders I deployed all over the world.

This is the case for most staff members today. As I talk to pastors across the country, most agree they have never been personally discipled. Most would not know what to do if they were asked to disciple anyone personally. They have been trained to lead church programs, preach, and offer pastoral care, but they don't know how to multiply themselves and raise up disciple-making leaders after them. Most people hired on church staffs in America today fit this scenario. They are amazing leaders, but they have never been discipled. They still operate to some degree under the superstar mentality, building their ministry instead of building leaders who will multiply. Thus, they limit their redemptive potential. Your greatest redemptive potential is not measured in what you can achieve alone but what can be achieved through you and those you train to multiply!

The second kind of leader I see in churches today is the disciple maker who never rises to leadership. Granted, not everyone is called to lead. Not everyone is gifted to lead (Rom. 12:8; 1 Cor. 12:28). However, over the years I have seen people with incredible potential for leadership never move into levels of leadership within the church for some reason. Sometimes that is by their own choice. Many have become disenfranchised with the local church to the point that they feel the only way to do effective ministry is to go around the church. Some have even gone so far as to devote most of their time to parachurch ministries that all too often are perceived as competing with the local church for leadership and resources. Others don't rise into church leadership because pastors are intimidated by these people. I've seen church leaders stiff-arm these would-be leaders because, quite frankly, they know how to make disciples more effectively than the church's staff. Pastors tend to overlook these qualified leaders and opt for those who will do things the way the pastor wants them done and not challenge the status quo.

In churches we find these two types of leaders: those who are leaders but not disciple makers, and those who are disciple makers but do not become leaders. But what we desperately need is a synthesis of the two: *disciple-making leaders*. We need men and women who lead out of the overflow of their walk with Christ and intentionally invest in others to produce genuine disciples and ministry leaders who will multiply into a movement.

This brings me back to the three businessmen who discipled me years ago. Although they were not on the church's staff, they held some of the highest leadership positions in the church. These men were revered and influential. They sat on church boards, championed vision initiatives, and personally led the way in hands-on ministry. They gave. They prayed. They loved deeply. They corrected when necessary. They earned the right to be heard and followed. Why? Because they were the real deal. They lived by example. They invested their lives. They poured into new leaders and taught them how to walk with God. And most important of all, they kept the church focused on its primary mission: to make disciples who make disciples to the ends of the earth.

THE URGENCY OF THE MATTER

We need more leaders like these three businessmen! We need churches full of them. We need church staffs full of them. We don't need more superstars; we need more disciple-making leaders. We don't need men and women who are limited by what only they can do; we need men and women who understand that their greatest potential lies in what can be achieved through those whom they train to multiply! Disciple-making leaders are the missing ingredient in the church today.

With every passing year, I feel an increasing urgency for these kinds of leaders because more than ever our times demand it. We are living in unprecedented, challenging times. We live in a culture that is divided and growing ever more hostile to the gospel. The lasting effects of the global pandemic are still yet to be seen.

I attended a small church planter "think tank" event in Chicago in the fall of 2019. One of the questions asked was this: How will churches survive if large gatherings are illegal in the United States? Such a question seemed theoretical at best, but none of us could have anticipated that within six months churches would be forced to close their doors across our country. What seemed theoretical had suddenly become very practical. As we reeled from the effects of the pandemic shutdown in our own church, my mind raced back to the solutions we had written on a whiteboard for such an occasion as this. Most of these solutions revolved around the idea of the decentralization of small groups. These groups would no longer meet in church buildings but rather in coffee shops, houses, apartment complexes, and offices.

However, for decentralized groups to work, a new brand of leader must be developed. This requires leaders who are self-sufficient in their walk with God. Leaders who can invest and train up other leaders with little to no oversight. And leaders who can multiply themselves, their groups, and other leaders at a rapid pace. In short, decentralization needs disciple-making leaders. Our times right now cry out for this new caliber of leader.

Another reason we need disciple-making leaders is because the gospel requires it. We won't reach the unreached in our communities and around the world with the number of leaders we have now. The short-sighted superstar might think, *Well, if my ministry is good, then everything is good.* But we know better. While a few churches are still growing at a minimal rate, the church in America is in decline. The old models and old strategies are inadequate for the new frontier ahead of us. How will we plant more churches unless we have more qualified leaders? How will we start new ministries without more qualified leaders? How will we multiply disciples without more qualified leaders? The short answer is we won't. Without multiplying leaders, the movement stops. That's why we must raise up new disciple-making leaders who will raise up more leaders to take the gospel to those who desperately need it.

YOUR GREATEST POTENTIAL

Let us not forget that Jesus commanded disciple making. If you go to the top of Mount Arbel along the western edge of the Sea of Galilee and stand on its peak, the Jezreel Valley stretches out before you like a patchwork quilt. From that vantage point, you can see glimpses of the nations of Syria and Jordan. On a clear day you can make out the chimney stacks of a power plant located next to ancient Caesarea Maritima, where the apostle Paul was kept in prison and later sent by ship to Rome. Most people believe this was where Jesus gave his Great Commission, his final command.

And with those last words, he did not say, "Go and make more leaders." He did not say, "Go and make more superstars." He said, "Go make disciples of all nations." Jesus' command was to make disciples who make disciples to the ends of the earth. But how will we do that if we do not have disciple-making leaders in our churches? Jesus trained twelve disciple-making leaders and commissioned them to make disciples and lead by example. As a result, twelve men turned the world upside down. It can happen again.

I started this chapter with a simple statement: every leader has potential, but not every leader reaches their potential. The pressing question is this: Are you reaching your maximum potential? Disciple-making leaders have known what you now know. Your greatest redemptive potential is not measured in what you alone can achieve but what can be achieved through you and those you train to multiply!

Before you press on, stop and ask yourself about your own leadership journey. Are you an experienced leader but have never been discipled? Are you a proven disciple maker but have never moved into a leadership role? What needs to change for you to maximize your potential as a disciple-making leader? In the next chapter we will take a deep dive into what Jesus had in mind when he commanded his early followers to make disciples and how you can follow his method of multiplying leaders around you.

GROUP DISCUSSION QUESTIONS

1. Do you know someone who had great potential but failed to reach it? Explain.
2. What is the definition of a disciple-making leader?
3. How would you describe the difference between a disciple-making leader and a typical leader?
4. Why are disciple-making leaders so important?
5. Would you describe yourself as a disciple-making leader? Why or why not?

DISCIPLE-MAKING MOVEMENT PROFILE

The Early Church Movement

Born in Tarsus of Cilicia between AD 1–4, in what is today the southeastern corner of Turkey, Saul was raised by devoted Jewish parents who taught him the Torah and held to a strict observance of the law. He was of the Hebrew tribe of Benjamin (Phil. 3:5–6) and as a young man was tutored by the rabbi Gamaliel (Acts 22:3). During this time, he developed a deep zeal for God's Word and a disdain for anything that threatened to contaminate or distract God's people from it. He trained as a lawyer and ultimately rose to the status of a Pharisee, the leading religious sect, which preached a strict obedience to God's law and personal piety. Saul's devotion to the Torah led him to participate in the early persecution of Christians. In fact, he stood in agreement as Stephen, the first Christian martyr, was killed (Acts 7:58). He even had the authorization to capture and imprison Christians because of their faith.

However, while on the road to Damascus in Syria, Saul encountered the risen Christ, an event that changed his life completely. A bright light blinded him, and he heard a voice say:

"Saul, Saul, why are you persecuting me?" (Acts 9:4). Saul asked who was speaking to him. The voice responded: "I am Jesus, the one you are persecuting" (Acts 9:5).

Saul was blinded because of this, and he arrived in Damascus in a state of shock. There a Christian named Ananias visited him after God had spoken to him about Saul: "Go, for this man is my chosen instrument to take my name to Gentiles, kings, and Israelites. I will show him how much he must suffer for my name" (Acts 9:15–16). Ananias prayed for Saul, placing his hands on him, and as he prayed, something like scales fell from Saul's eyes, and he regained his sight.

Soon thereafter, he began to preach openly in Damascus that Jesus was the long-awaited Messiah (Acts 9:22).

Upon leaving Damascus, Saul spent time in Arabia and later Jerusalem, confirming his newfound faith in Jesus with the Scriptures. Later, he embarked on three missionary journeys to preach the gospel among the Gentiles and plant churches. While he was often referred to by his Jewish name, Saul, he later preferred to use his Roman name, Paul, to communicate better to a Gentile audience (Acts 13:9).

Paul's methodology was simple and often repeated. After he entered a town, he sought out the Jewish synagogue (Acts 13:5, 14; 14:1; 18:19), where he preached the gospel. Many were curious and wanted to hear more. However, over time, the religious leaders opposed Paul and his message. This opposition often became violent, leading to riots, beatings, stoning, or imprisonment. As a result of his public preaching of the gospel, true believers gathered in that town and formed the nucleus of a church. Once a church was established, Paul remained in the city, teaching and instructing them in the gospel, training leaders, and installing elders and pastors (Acts 19:8–10). This training took place both in large group settings as well as personal investments.

Paul writes to Timothy, "What you have heard from me in the presence of many witnesses, commit to faithful men who will be able to teach others also" (2 Tim. 2:2*)*. This gives us insight into Paul's strategy for multiplication. First, his plan was highly relational. Just as he had entrusted the gospel to Timothy and trained him up in the faith, Timothy was to do the same with faithful, reliable men. Second, Paul's plan envisioned generational growth. One generation of disciples was obligated to train and release the next generation to reproduce. In this passage we see four generations pictured: Paul, Timothy, faithful men, and future disciples. Last, Paul's plan was intentional. This kind of personal investment would produce multiplying disciple makers who would plant churches and advance the kingdom of God.

Once Paul established churches and leaders, he often followed up with them personally and encouraged them in the faith (Acts 14:21–23). He also left them epistles, sacred divinely inspired texts, exhorting them in doctrine and practice (Col. 4:16; 2 Tim. 3:16–17). Young leaders such as Timothy, Titus, John Mark, Aquila and Priscilla, Epaphras, Luke, Lucius, Jason, Sosipater, Tertius, Gaius, and others were trained by Paul and sent out to preach the gospel, plant churches, and pastor congregations. In this way, Paul followed the model of Jesus, and he spread the gospel throughout Asia Minor and Europe and all over the world (Col. 1:6).

2

THE PRIORITY

I'll never forget sitting in my office, staring at the folder on my desk. I could feel the anxiety welling up in me, producing a knot in the pit of my stomach. I had been the pastor of this church for three years, and in that time the church had not experienced any substantial growth. During my first year I was convinced I knew how to get the stalled church moving again. But now, after emptying my bag of tricks, the church remained as it had been, steady but stagnant.

So I met with a church consultant for advice. He said, "Don't worry, Craig. I'll do a CAT scan of your church and find out what's going on." That sounded promising, and I hoped he would find something I had overlooked. For the next several months this man met with our staff, interviewed leaders, gathered focus groups, analyzed data, and assessed our church from top to bottom.

Ultimately, he produced the report that now sat on my desk. I heard the clock ticking in the otherwise silent room. I thought, *This could be good news. Maybe he has found a few things we can change quickly that will get us growing again.* But those thoughts were quickly nudged aside by fearful thoughts. *What if it's bad news? What if nothing can be done? What if the church is stuck? What if I'm stuck?* I took a deep breath and opened the folder.

The report confirmed my worst fears. While our church had excellent programs and facilities, the future was not optimistic. Because the church did not reflect the community, the conclusion was that apart from a relocation the church would ultimately struggle and die. I remember the consultant's words, "You are swimming upstream and eventually you will wear out." Those words landed like a gut punch. I closed the report and slipped to my knees. Then face down on the floor, I began to pray. "Lord, what do you want me to do? I don't know what to do next. Surely you didn't call me here simply to hold the hand of a dying church. I know this is not your dream for this church, but I don't know what to do."

That was my worst moment of desperation.

An intense season of prayer followed. Our staff met early in the morning to pray. We called on godly men in our church to pray with us and seek the Lord for direction. Through this time of soul searching, I realized one of our greatest problems was I had not prioritized making disciples. I had aggressively pursued the latest church ministry models. I had constantly sought out what other churches did and tried to adapt their methods to our church's context, but I had not really considered Jesus' life as my model for ministry.

Of course, I had heard the Great Commission many times. I had preached it. But I had not taken to heart the simple fact that in those verses Jesus had commanded me and every church to make disciples. This was his priority. This was his compelling cause. This was (and still is today) the primary work of his church. In fact, he gave the promise of his presence to any church that prioritized this one command. Unfortunately, my greatest failure was trying to grow the church without making disciples.

JESUS' CLEAR PRIORITY

On three different occasions Jesus clarified his disciples' mission:

- "All authority has been given to me in heaven and on earth. Go, therefore, and make disciples of all nations, baptizing them in the name of the Father and of the Son and of the Holy Spirit, teaching them to observe everything I have commanded you.

And remember, I am with you always, to the end of the age" (Matt. 28:18–20).

- "Go into all the world and preach the gospel to all creation. Whoever believes and is baptized will be saved, but whoever does not believe will be condemned" (Mark 16:15–16).
- "But you will receive power when the Holy Spirit has come on you, and you will be my witnesses in Jerusalem, in all Judea and Samaria, and to the ends of the earth" (Acts 1:8).

Just looking at these three verses, Jesus' priority becomes crystal clear. Jesus wanted his disciples to make disciples of all nations. They were to do this by preaching the gospel and calling people to respond in faith; baptizing these new believers; training them to live obediently to God; then sending them out to make disciples, starting at home and extending to the ends of the earth. If you had asked his disciples, "What mattered most to Jesus?" I'm sure they would have answered, "Making disciples who multiply was his clear priority."

Now let me ask you something, and really think about this. Is making disciples your clear priority? Is making disciples what gets rewarded in your ministry? Are those who make disciples the ones who get promoted and recognized in your church?

IS MAKING DISCIPLES YOUR CLEAR PRIORITY?

SAME WORDS, DIFFERENT LANGUAGE

Years ago, I received an invitation to meet with several national discipleship leaders. If I mentioned their names, you would know them. Most of them had written extensively about discipleship for decades and led national disciple-making ministries. Honestly, I'm not even sure why I was in the room. I felt like a kid invited to sit at the adult table for the first time.

Once the meeting started, the conversation turned to making disciples. The question came up, "How do you define a disciple?" Everyone jumped in like a pack of dogs on a bone, and soon the conversation turned into a heated debate. Before long, sharp words were being tossed across the table like verbal bombs. I couldn't believe what I saw. Here were the top minds in North America on discipleship, and we couldn't agree on a simple definition.

Finally, Bill Hull stood to his feet. His six-foot-seven frame towered over everyone who was seated. Bill had pastored churches for years before serving in denominational leadership. However, over the past three decades, he has probably been the most prolific writer and speaker on the topic of discipleship. His works are the gold standard for understanding biblical disciple making.

Everyone in the room had the highest respect for Bill, so when he raised his hands in a gesture to quiet the crowd, the room fell silent. "Gentlemen," he said in a calm tone with a gentle smile, "we are using the same words, but we are speaking a different language." He was right. Everyone was using the word "disciple" but meaning something different. I find that to be the case just about every time I gather to talk about disciple making with pastors. Everyone agrees that we should make disciples. Everyone agrees that churches should produce disciples, but not everyone agrees on the definition of a disciple.

So how do you define a "disciple"?

WHAT IS A DISCIPLE?

If you look back to Mathew 28:19, you read: "Go, therefore, and make disciples of all nations." The Greek word for "disciple" is *mathetes*, which is used 230 times in the Gospels and twenty-eight times in the book of Acts. It means "to learn" or "to be a learner." This word was the predominant term used to describe a follower of Jesus. The Hebrew word *talmid* is an equivalent term. A *talmid* was a learner, usually one enrolled in training to become a rabbi. Ray Vander Laan explains:

> The Hebrew word for disciple is *talmid*. This word stresses the relationship between rabbi (teacher or master) and disciple (student). A *talmid* of Jesus' day would give up his entire life to be

> with his teacher. The disciple didn't only seek to know what the teacher knew, as is usually the case today. It was not enough just to know what the rabbi said, but the foremost goal of any *talmid* was to become like the rabbi and do what the rabbi did.[8]

But the ancient idea of being a disciple was far more than just acquiring knowledge or even accumulating credentials, as in the case of modern higher education. A disciple was to become like their teacher, to match the model of their teacher, and to carry on the teacher's work long after the teacher was gone.

Thus, a mature disciple of Jesus isn't one who just claims to know Jesus by way of salvation; rather, a mature disciple becomes more and more like him in every way.

This is the end goal of the Christian disciple's life: Christlikeness.

The apostle Paul communicates this idea many times in his epistles. For example, Philippians 2:5 says, "Adopt the same attitude as that of Christ Jesus." The term "attitude" (*phroneo*) means an inner disposition and outer behavior. The disciple of Jesus is to think inwardly and act outwardly like Jesus. This imitation of Jesus has always been the goal of true disciples, which Paul expresses: "Imitate me, as I also imitate Christ" (1 Cor. 11:1). The term "imitate" comes from the Greek word *mimetes*, which means to mimic the actions of another person. Paul calls his followers to mimic his life as he mimics the life of Jesus.

Also, in Romans 8:29, Paul says, "For those he foreknew he also predestined to be conformed to the image of his Son, so that he would be the firstborn among many brothers and sisters." So immediately after declaring that God works all things together for the good of those who love him and are called to his higher purpose, Paul states that God's endgame for every believer is to be "conformed to the image of his Son." That is, to look more and more like Jesus. This is what it means to be a mature disciple of Jesus: wanting what he wants, loving what he loves, having the same perspective he has, grieving over what grieves him, and being committed to the same things to which he was committed.

One of the clearest understandings of this is found in the "just as" statements of Jesus in John's Gospel. Jesus often used the phrase "just as" to indicate the similarity of himself and his true followers. Just as he was dependent on his Father, his true disciples would be dependent on him (John 6:57). Just as Jesus served in humility, his true disciples would follow his example of humble service (John 13:15). Just as Jesus loved them, his true disciples would love one another (John 13:34). Just as Jesus did great works, his true disciples would do greater works (John 14:12). Just as Jesus kept the commands of his Father and remained in his love, his true disciples would keep his commands and remain in his love (John 15:10). And just as the Father sent him, Jesus would send his true disciples into the world with the gospel (John 20:21). Living as a disciple of Jesus means living as Jesus did. Therefore 1 John 2:6 says, "Whoever claims to live in him must live as Jesus lived" (NIV).

Recently, several writers have referred to an ancient phrase that describes a disciple as being "covered in the dust" of his teacher. The phrase originates from the Mishnah, the Jewish oral traditions collected as the first words of rabbinic literature, written between 200 BC and AD 200. We read in Avot 1:4, "Let thy house be a meeting house for the wise; and powder thyself in the dust of their feet; and drink their words with thirstiness." Scholars attribute this quote to Rabbi Yose ben Yoezer, who predated Jesus by two hundred years.

"The wise" in Rabbi Yose ben Yoezer's time were itinerate preachers and teachers, and they were precursors to "rabbis," a term which originated in approximately AD 70. So "to powder thyself in the dust of [a rabbi's] feet" could have two meanings. One is the idea of sitting at the feet of these rabbis and learning from them. We see this throughout the Scriptures as the posture of a disciple. For example, Jesus as a young boy sat in the temple at the feet of his teachers (Luke 2:46), and the apostle Paul was "educated at the feet of Gamaliel" (Acts 22:3). Mary sat and learned at the feet of Jesus (Luke 10:39), and the demoniac, after his miraculous deliverance, sat at the feet of Jesus as a disciple (Luke 8:35). So this obscure phrase in the ancient Mishnah could be an instruction for a disciple to sit at the feet of a rabbi to learn.

But how would sitting at a rabbi's feet result in being "powdered" by his dust? That leads to the second meaning, which pictures these disciples following so closely behind their rabbi along the road that they walked through the dust clouds stirred by the rabbi's feet, therefore "powdering" themselves in the dust of his feet. Unlike today where classes take place in classrooms, the ancients trained as they walked along the road and completed menial daily tasks. Whether disciples sat or walked, they were always to remain within the orbit of their master's dust and teaching.[9]

This was the passion of a *mathetes*. This was the call of a true disciple of Jesus Christ, to follow him and to become like him.

THREE-DIMENSIONAL

Jesus' favorite invitation was "follow me." The Greek word *akoloutheo* is used over ninety times in the Scriptures. In one sense, the word means to be a companion along the road, but it can also indicate the devotion of a disciple. *Thayer's Greek-English Lexicon of the New Testament* adds this definition: "To join one as a disciple, become or be his disciple; side with his party (Matthew 4:20, 22; Matthew 9:9; Matthew 19:27; Mark 1:18; Mark 8:34), . . . to cleave steadfastly to one, conform wholly to his example, in living and if need be in dying also (Matthew 10:38; Matthew 16:24; John 12:26; John 21:22)."[10]

Jesus extended this invitation to Peter and Andrew, James and John as they mended their nets by the Sea of Galilee: "Follow me, . . . and I will make you fish for people" (Matt. 4:19). He gave the same invitation to Philip from Bethsaida (John 1:43), to the casual observers (Luke 9:59–62), and to the rich young ruler (Mark 10:21). Jesus never pressured people to follow him. He never pushed or threatened. He simply invited them to come and be his disciples. Some did. Some didn't.

What does being a disciple of Jesus resemble today? In ancient times, following a master was profoundly tangible. It meant leaving a business of fishing, farming, or construction and devoting yourself completely to following a teacher and learning from him. But how do we do that today? Obviously, we can't physically follow Jesus around. Over the years I've found it helpful to develop a simple definition of a disciple that could be easily used as a benchmark for spiritual growth. This definition is not exhaustive by far. Trust me, I've developed long lists of discipleship behaviors, only to watch the blood drain from people's faces when they think they are expected to live up to such a standard. Simpler is better.

Here are three simple words to describe a growing disciple. I call this the 3D disciple. When an object is in 3D, it's three-dimensional, fully orbed, fully formed. And when a disciple is mature, they will have these three characteristics:

A mature disciple devotes themself to Jesus. To be a follower of Jesus is to be devoted to Jesus. In the book of Acts, we see followers of Jesus (Luke 22:49) synonymous with true believers (Acts 4:32). And these "believers" are also referred to as "disciples" (Acts 6:2). Later, these disciples of Jesus are called "Christians" for the first time (Acts 11:26). In the epistles we see other terms used to describe followers of Jesus, such as "saint" (2 Cor. 1:1); "elect" (1 Pet. 1:1, NIV); and "children of God" (1 John 3:1).

All these terms indicate a sincere devotion to Jesus (2 Cor. 11:3). To be devoted to Christ means to have recognized one's sin, heard the gospel, and responded in faith and repentance, as seen in Jesus' first sermon: "The time is fulfilled, and the kingdom of God has come near. Repent and believe the good news" (Mark 1:15, see also Acts 2:38; 16:31). So the first indication of a true disciple is one's devotion to Jesus exemplified in their repentance of sin and their faith in Christ alone for forgiveness and salvation.

A mature disciple develops in the character and competencies of Jesus. Once a person professes their faith in Christ, evidence of spiritual growth and development should exist. Living things grow. And a newly born-again child of God will grow in the likeness of Jesus. Peter has this in mind when he writes, "Like newborn infants, desire the pure milk of the word, so that by it you may grow up into your salvation" (1 Pet. 2:2). So every true believer is a growing believer.

Jesus put it this way: "Everyone when he is fully trained will be like his teacher" (Luke 6:40, ESV). This training in Christlikeness produces both internal change (the change of one's character, values, beliefs, and desires) and external change (godly behavior, skills, and competencies that foster ongoing spiritual growth and multiplication). Most people think of discipleship as helping another learn to read their Bible, memorize Scripture, share their faith, learn to resist temptation, and serve God in their giftedness. This is the ongoing spiritual growth of every believer. Therefore, the second indication of a mature disciple is the evidence of spiritual growth and change.

A mature disciple deploys themself into the mission of Jesus. When a soldier is deployed, he leaves the comfort of home and ventures into enemy territory to fulfill the mission of his commanding officer. And when a true disciple is deployed, he goes about the mission of Jesus.

On his last night with his disciples, Jesus reminded them of their mission. Traversing the Kidron Valley, headed to the Garden of Gethsemane, they walked through a vineyard. Jesus paused to teach a lesson about abiding in him. He said, "By this my Father is glorified, that you bear much fruit and so prove to be my disciples" (John 15:8, ESV). What brings the Father glory? What proves to the world that someone is a true disciple of Jesus? Bearing fruit—lasting fruit, eternal fruit—by walking with God, reaching their world, and investing in a few. This is as true today as it was for Jesus' original disciples. True disciples prove their faith when they are deployed into the mission field.

Using this simple 3D tool has helped me quickly assess someone's spiritual growth and help them take the next step toward Jesus. A true disciple devotes themself to Jesus, which means they can articulate a time when they came to faith in Jesus, they can communicate their testimony, and they have likely been baptized. This disciple also develops in their relationship with Christ. They are connected to a local church, enjoying biblical community with other believers, and growing in their love for God and people. At the same time, they experience some kind of internal change. Their character becomes more and more like Jesus. They hate what God hates and love what God loves. Along the way, they become less focused on themselves and more focused on others. They also develop a heart to serve people both inside and outside the church. Last, a true disciple deploys themself into the mission of Jesus. They share their faith with the people at their workplace or in their neighborhood. They invest in others and show them how to walk with God, reach their world, and invest in a few. They give, sacrifice, and work to advance God's kingdom at home and around the world. This is the kind of disciple Jesus called us to make. This is the work to which Jesus calls each of us.

DO THE WORKS

Making disciples of Jesus is the work of ministry. C. S. Lewis, the great author and philosopher, writes:

> The Church exists for nothing else but to draw men into Christ, to make them little Christs. If they are not doing that, all the cathedrals, clergy, missions, sermons, even the Bible itself, are simply a waste of time. God became Man for no other purpose. It is even doubtful, you know, whether the whole universe was created for any other purpose.[11]

This is why Jesus came to earth. This is why all creation stood still as the Son of God came in human flesh, walked among us, endured the cross, and rose in power. He did it to draw men to himself and make them like himself.

Producing this kind of fully mature disciple was also the passion of the apostle Paul. He writes, "We proclaim him, warning and teaching everyone with all wisdom, so that we may present everyone mature in Christ. I labor for this, striving with his strength that works powerfully in me" (Col. 1:28–29). This work was a labor of love and required warning and teaching others. It also required effort. Yes, investing your life will cost you. Moving people toward spiritual maturity will cost you, but Paul didn't strive alone in his own fleshly efforts because the Spirit empowered him. And when you invest your life in others and help them walk toward maturity, you partner, arm in arm, with the Spirit's work.

Ministry is not just the work of recruiting volunteers, executing excellent programming, building new facilities, preaching sermons, and offering pastoral care, counseling, and compassionate ministries. Ministry is not just managing budgets, meetings, and events. Ministry is not just paperwork, administrative duties, and operational leadership. At its core, ministry is making disciples. Ministry is changing lives by investing personally in others. Ministry is seeing people respond to the gospel. Ministry is helping those same people grow in Jesus and reflect him more clearly. Ministry is sending his people into the world to fulfill his mission where they live, learn, work, and play. This is the work of the church. This is the work of every ministry leader. And this is your primary work. This is the joyful work to which you have dedicated your life. It is your single objective as commanded by Jesus. And it is the only work that will last long after you are gone.

MINISTRY IS SENDING JESUS' PEOPLE INTO THE WORLD TO FULFILL HIS MISSION.

On one occasion, Jesus was with his disciples when they spotted a blind man. Seeing the man in obvious suffering, begging for bread from the passing masses, the disciples asked, "Rabbi, who sinned, this man or his parents, that he was born blind?" Surely someone was to blame for this man's condition. Why else would he be in this sad state? But Jesus said something none of them expected. "Neither this man nor his parents sinned. . . . This came about so that God's works might be displayed in him." In other words, this man's condition was not a result of personal sin but providence. God wanted to use the upcoming transformation as a tool to display his glory and goodness. Then Jesus said: "We must do the works of him who sent me while it is day. Night is coming when no one can work" (John 9:1–4). Then Jesus spat on the ground, mixed it with dirt, placed the mud on the man's eyes, and told him to wash in the pool of Siloam. The man obeyed Jesus and came back seeing for the first time. Just like that, his life was changed. Jesus had used dirt and spit and human hands to transform this man's life and bring glory to God.

Every day we see people in pain. This fallen world takes a toll on us all. We see marriages in shambles. We see families frayed at the edges. We see addiction, crime, hate, sexual sin, and deep-rooted shame from the past. But through it all God brings himself glory by transforming people's lives. And how does he do it? He uses ordinary things, ordinary people like you and like me. God is working in someone's life, and you can play a part. God is writing a new story in someone's life, and you get to contribute a line. God is orchestrating a miracle in someone's life, and you have a role to play. As you "do the works" of making disciples, you join in God's great work of redemption and transformation, one life at a time.

Thinking back to reading that report in my office, God used that moment of desperation to lead me back to his top priority, making disciples. Over the years that followed, the church and I committed to defining a disciple, and then relentlessly investing in people who would do the same. We gave ourselves to the work of disciple making and God blessed us. The church that had a dismal prognosis, according to the consultant, began to grow. We invested in a few people who in turn began to disciple others. As the church leadership matured, they began to think more outward than inward. We started ministering to local, inner-city schools, at first providing clothes for students and resources for campus projects, but soon we earned their trust and began leading Bible studies and sharing the gospel. Hundreds of students gave their lives to Christ. We planted churches in our area, launched a new campus, and built a facility to care for kids in our community.

I don't have to time to tell you all God did through that church. All I can say is God did something no one could have predicted because we took seriously his priority to make disciples. Are you asking God to do great things in your church? Are you longing for God to move in incredible ways? God works powerfully in a church that is committed to doing his work. God displays his presence powerfully in any church that does what he called them to do: to make disciples who make disciples to the ends of the earth.

GROUP DISCUSSION QUESTIONS

1. How would you describe the culture of your current ministry setting?
2. What are the key elements of a disciple-making culture?
3. How do you define a disciple?
4. Which of the three elements in the 3D definition of a disciple stands out the most to you? Why?
5. What keeps most churches from being focused on the priority of making disciples?

DISCIPLE-MAKING MOVEMENT PROFILE

The Patristic Movement

Ignatius was the bishop of the church in Antioch, Syria, one of the largest and most prominent in its day. We know very little about him. His wide-reaching and fruitful ministry is lost in time. Ignatius was born five years after the death of Christ and lived his life for Christ during a time of tremendous worldwide persecution.

Arrested in Antioch, most likely for refusing to bow to the pagan Roman gods, he was bound and transported to Rome for trial and execution. Along the way he wrote letters to churches he visited, namely Ephesus, Magnesia, Tralles, Philadelphia, and Smyrna. He also penned letters, with the help of a scribe, to his friend Polycarp, of the church of Smyrna, and one to the church at Rome, who planned to receive him and attempt to negotiate his release. However, he had no desire to be released but desired to give himself as a martyr for Christ. "I fear your kindness, which may harm me," he wrote to Roman Christians hoping to free him. "You may be able to achieve what you plan. But if you pay no heed to my request, it will be very difficult for me to attain unto God."[12]

Ignatius stands out among the apostolic fathers for his frequent use of the term "disciple." Ignatius used the term "discipleship" fourteen times in his letters, whereas all the other apostolic fathers combined to use the term a dozen times. For Ignatius, the term "disciple" had three main usages. First, a disciple designated a person who was a Christian. Second, it identified a person growing in their commitment to Christ. Therefore, "to make a disciple" was an expression like that of Jesus' command in Matthew 28:18–20 to make disciples. And last, it connoted a Christian martyr. Ignatius did not believe martyrdom itself was a work rendered for salvation, but it was a full expression of discipleship in that it most imitated Jesus, who died on our behalf.

His thoughts on martyrdom are difficult to grasp fully today, yet they give us insight into the devotion of a disciple of Jesus in a hostile world:

> Now at last I am beginning to be a disciple. May nothing visible or invisible envy me, so that I may reach Jesus Christ. Fire and cross and battles with wild beasts, mutilation, mangling, wrenching of bones, the hacking of limbs, the crushing of my whole body, cruel tortures of the devil—let these come upon me, only let me reach Jesus Christ! (Rom. 5.1.4–5.3.3)[13]

For Ignatius, discipleship was the Christian life. To embrace Jesus was to embrace a life of discipleship. He wrote, "Having become his disciples, let us learn to live in accordance with Christianity. For whoever is called by any other name than this does not belong to God" (Ign. Mag. 10.1.3).[14] Devotion to Christ is evidenced by faithfulness, obedience, and endurance. This is especially true for Christians experiencing persecution. In the time of Ignatius, if one was charged with being a Christian, they could simply deny Christ and be released. But those who were devoted to Jesus didn't disown him, even if it meant imprisonment or death.

The apostolic fathers also understood discipleship to be a developmental process, beginning when one comes to faith in Jesus and continuing throughout a lifetime. Mature believers are to model a Christlike life for new believers to follow. According to *The Martyrdom of Polycarp,* one who is influenced by another believer is said to be a disciple of that person.[15] And this radical devotion to Christ passed on from one to another in a disciple-making relationship that caused the church to multiply rapidly.

3

THE PATHWAY

When you lose your why, you lose your way. This is true on so many levels. When you lose the why of your purpose, you lose your way and seek purpose in lesser things. When you lose the why of your marriage, you lose your way and drift into selfishness or cynicism. When you lose your why in ministry, you lose your way and seek to satisfy yourself with things that do not last. And this is certainly the case when it comes to making disciples. When a church loses its why—when it forgets that its primary purpose is to make disciples—then it loses its way.

A pilot once shared with me the "sixty to one" rule in aviation. If a pilot is off just one degree from his directional heading, he will drift one mile off course for every sixty miles he travels. For example, if I were to fly from Fort Lauderdale, Florida, to Tampa, Florida, and the pilot was off just one degree from his directional heading, I would miss Tampa by just a little over three miles. That's certainly not too far to make a course correction and land in Tampa. But if I were flying from Fort Lauderdale, Florida, to Honolulu, Hawaii, and the pilot was off by just one degree, I would miss the island by eighty-one miles. That means I would be swimming somewhere in the middle of the Pacific Ocean looking for a runway.

Jesus set the directional heading of the church when he gave us our mission to "make disciples of all nations," yet the more the church has ignored his command, the further it has drifted from his intended purpose. Across America we are witnessing today how the church is off course. Churches are losing their way into doctrinal errors, losing their way into unbiblical social activism, losing their way into cultural conformity on multiple levels, and losing their way into busyness with no result in mind. And what do we have to show for it? Little life change and few transformed. We have drifted from our heading, and we are paying the price to the point that many churches today would be completely unrecognizable from that of the early church. I have a friend who says, "Jesus started the church the way he wanted it. Now he wants it the way he started it."

In the previous chapter we discovered Jesus' priority of disciple making. The question now becomes, how do we do that? In this chapter we will dive into the disciple-making pathway Jesus used to make multiplying disciples who would ultimately ignite a global movement.

INTENTIONAL JESUS

Jesus did everything with a purpose. While some read the Gospels and assume Jesus just wandered aimlessly from town to town, preaching and healing, the exact opposite is true. He chose every step and calculated every move. He knew what he was doing and where he was going.

If you travel to Israel today and visit the hometown of Jesus, you'll find it drastically different than it was two thousand years ago. Today the streets are congested with buses and taxis, while pedestrians busily crisscross the narrow sidewalks. The calls to prayer ring throughout the city at their appointed hours from the mosque minarets that contour the skyline. Over 77,000 people call Nazareth their home today, but in the time of Jesus it was a small, sleepy village of only a few hundred.

On the southern side of town is a steep precipice that overlooks the Jezreel Valley, which takes my breath away every time I see it. I can imagine Jesus sitting there, looking over the valley, when one day his Father said it was time to begin his earthly ministry. From there he traveled south, down the Jordan River Valley to "Bethany across the Jordan," where John the Baptist baptized him (John 1:28). At that point, the clock started ticking. He knew his time was short. He had no time for detours or delays. He began his ministry with a laser-like focus and determination, setting in motion a strategy that would ultimately produce men who changed the world.

Most ministry leaders today are unaware of this strategy of Jesus. And I was certainly one of them. I never heard of Jesus' strategy growing up in church. I never heard it discussed during my time in college or seminary. I was well into my first pastoring position when I met men who knew the strategy of Jesus. They spoke of it as if everyone knew what they were talking about, but I didn't.

One of these men, Dann Spader, encouraged me to buy *The NIV Harmony of the Gospels*.[16] This book takes the four Gospels (Mathew, Mark, Luke, and John) and places them in chronological order. After reading the book, I saw what Jesus did in year one, year two, and year three. I saw moves Jesus made and patterns he developed that were far from haphazard and clearly strategic. Today that *Harmony of the Gospels* is well worn. Its pages are folded, margins scribbled, the binding has been reinforced with clear packing tape. It's like a well-worn glove, an old friend. Yet it still brings new insight into this strategy of Jesus.

So what is this strategy? How does it apply to making disciples today?

THIRTY THOUSAND FEET

Looking out the window of an airplane yields perspective. Everything below looks so small. And from that distance you can see the larger topographical structures that were unnoticeable from ground level. The same is true with Jesus' strategy. Before we dive into the details, let's first pull up and take a thirty-thousand-foot view to see the big pieces of his strategy and how they fit together.

The best place to begin is with Jesus' words from Mount Arbel. We find them in Matthew's Gospel:

> All authority has been given to me in heaven and on earth. Go, therefore, and make disciples of all nations, baptizing them in

> the name of the Father and of the Son and of the Holy Spirit, teaching them to observe everything I have commanded you. And remember, I am with you always, to the end of the age. (Matt. 28:18–20)

As I mentioned in the last chapter, the focal command of this passage is to "make disciples." You might want to circle those two words to keep them in your sights. The church exists to make disciples. To put it another way, disciples are the product of the church. However, supportive phrases in this passage reveal the process by which disciples are made. So in one sentence, Jesus revealed both the product and the process. This underscores the brilliance and intentionality of Jesus.

THE CHURCH EXISTS TO MAKE DISCIPLES.

Remember, Jesus gave this command to his men *after* his resurrection from the dead. They had already been through this process, so now he summarized it for them so they would never forget. What is this strategic process?

The first step in Jesus' strategy is simply to engage spiritual explorers. "Go, therefore, and make disciples." You can't spell "gospel" without first spelling "go." This indicates that the first step in disciple making is evangelism, taking the gospel to those who have not yet heard of Jesus. On occasion, someone will challenge me on the importance of making disciples, insisting that evangelism was Jesus' primary objective. This is understandable because we often separate evangelism and discipleship into separate categories. Most see evangelism as leading people to Jesus and discipleship as growing people in Jesus. Sounds good, right? Some even say, "I'm more into evangelism," or, "I'm more into discipleship." But choosing preferences like this isn't biblical. In fact, the words "evangelism" and "discipleship" are not even found in the Bible. In Jesus' mind, making disciples included declaring the good news as well as helping people grow in their faith to the point that they can reproduce. So disciple making begins with evangelism and ends with evangelism.

Jesus' strategy begins with going to those who need the gospel. In fact, some called Jesus a "friend of . . . sinners" (Matt. 11:19) which was meant to be a putdown, but Jesus wore it as a badge of honor. He came to seek and save the lost (Luke 19:10). Jesus told his disciples, "As the Father has sent me, I also send you" (John 20:21). So the first step is to engage spiritual explorers, to take the gospel to people who want to explore God and are open to hear the truth.

The second step in Jesus' strategy is to connect believers: "Baptizing them in the name of the Father and of the Son and of the Holy Spirit." Once a person comes to Christ, then they are welcomed into the family of God, and this begins with baptism. But baptism also is a demonstration of their identification with Jesus and inclusion into the church. When a person is baptized, they "go public" in their relationship with Jesus and declare to be his disciple. Therefore, from the very beginning, baptism was how new believers were connected to the fellowship of Christ followers.

Think about the birth of a child. That little life comes into the world, and it's a miraculous event. You see the wonder and the wisdom of God through it all, taking two people and producing a new life that is a mixture of the two. And what happens immediately afterward? The child receives a name and becomes part of a family. The hospital room fills with parents and grandparents, aunts and uncles, and nieces and nephews all gathering around this newborn baby. The child doesn't know it yet, but they will need this family. This family will nurture, protect, and train up this little one.

And the same is true when someone comes to faith in Jesus. They receive a new identity in Christ. They are a new creation after they experience the miracle of the "new birth" (John 3:3). However, this new believer also needs a family to nurture them spiritually, encourage them, and protect them from evil influences that seek to pull them away from their newfound faith. So Jesus said we not only need to go to those who are spiritually exploring, but we also need to lead them to faith in Jesus and root them in a faith family that will raise them up in the Lord.

The third step in Jesus' strategy is to grow disciples: "Teaching them to observe everything I have commanded you." After a person hears the gospel and responds to Christ in faith, is baptized and connected to a church, they can grow in their faith. They must be taught how to obey Jesus. When people read this passage, they often emphasize the word "teaching," which is why so much emphasis is on teaching in churches today. Certainly, teaching is an integral part of the Christian's spiritual growth. However, Jesus didn't emphasize teaching as much as obeying. Jesus sought obedience, which requires training.

Later in the New Testament, Paul tells Timothy, "Train yourself in godliness" (1 Tim. 4:7). Training is vital to spiritual growth. Think about any professional athlete—their life is committed to training. They train for years so they can compete at the highest level. Think about the soldier who trains for years so they are ready to fight. In the same way, if a person is to grow up spiritually, they need train in both the character and competencies of Jesus. This training includes how to feed yourself spiritually, how to study God's Word, how to share your faith, how to be faithful in prayer, how to stand against temptation, how to invest your life in others, etc. In short, this is training in how to follow Jesus.

The final step in Jesus' strategic plan is to multiply disciple makers. Look at his words again: "Teaching them to observe everything I have commanded you." New believers are to be taught to obey all his commands, but what command had Jesus just given them? To make disciples. So embedded in their obedience is the expectation to multiply. Jesus wanted every follower to be fully trained to be a multiplying disciple maker. This is what happened in the book of Acts as we read of the rapid multiplication of the church. Acts 6:7 says, "The disciples multiplied greatly" (ESV). These early Christians quickly multiplied and spread the gospel throughout Jerusalem and the known world.

Look at this four-step process for making disciples one more time: 1) engage spiritual explorers; 2) connect believers; 3) grow disciples; and 4) multiply disciple makers.

THE DISCIPLE-MAKING PATHWAY

Explore — Connect — Grow — Multiply

At first glance, this plan seemed too simple. Surely there was a more impressive way. But its simplicity is revolutionary because it transcends time, cultures, borders, languages, and customs. This is how the early church grew in the face of brutal opposition and pluralism and how the church today continues to thrive under totalitarian regimes and militant persecution. Despite the technological advancements and sophistication of our day, this simple strategy continues to transform lives with the gospel.

Before moving on, let me mention a few important aspects of this strategic plan. First, Jesus' plan is sequential. That is, one phase builds on the next. A person must be engaged with the gospel before coming to faith in Christ and connecting in biblical community. Then a person must find meaningful connection in community before truly beginning to be trained spiritually. And this training is vitally necessary before a person can reproduce in a healthy, productive way. Each step is important and necessary.

Some argue that this process is too restrictive. "After all," they say, "each person grows at their own pace and in their own way." But is that true? Think about how a child grows. Every child is different and unique; not one is the same. Yet every child develops in the same predictable way to the degree that pediatricians can tell if a child is developing properly and at the proper rate. A child is unique, but the process is not. The same is true in spiritual growth. While each person's transformation is unique, their journey runs along predictable patterns. Of course, the details are different. How and when a person comes to Christ and finds fellowship in a church family will look very different, but the steps of spiritual growth are predictably the same.

Jesus alluded to this when he said:

> The kingdom of God is like this. . . . A man scatters seed on the ground. He sleeps and rises night and day; the seed sprouts and grows, although he doesn't know how. The soil produces a crop by itself—first the blade, then the head, and then the full grain on the head. As soon as the crop is ready, he sends for the sickle, because the harvest has come. (Mark 4:26–29)

Jesus said the kingdom of God is growing, advancing. But it grows much like a stalk of wheat. First is the blade, then the head, then the full grain. I worked for a seed company when I was in high school. We traveled all throughout South Texas harvesting sorghum crops and testing their yields. I learned that these plants are all unique, but they all grow the same way. Thus, while we like to think we are so special that we can build our own spiritual-growth process, Jesus has the perfect process already in place. And when we think we can skip a step in that process, we do so at our own peril.

On some occasions I have thought, *I don't think this person really needs this next step. I'll just skip it and move on.* Each time I do that, I regret it. The product is never the same. My wife is a master cook. In fact, it's hard to lose weight at my house because everything she makes is so good. And when she makes a new dish, she meticulously follows the recipe. She does not vary or improvise because she knows the creator of the dish knows what is necessary at each stage to produce the desired result. In the same way, Jesus is the master disciple maker. Neither you nor I can improve on his process. Rather, we must follow his lead.

Second, this process is supernatural. In each step of this process, God is at work, growing and developing you. Remember Paul's words in Colossians 1:28–29, "We proclaim him, warning and teaching everyone with all wisdom, so that we may present everyone mature in Christ. I labor for this, striving with his strength that works powerfully in me." Paul knew that while he labored, the Spirit of God brought about change. So it's humbling to know that when Jesus calls us to make disciples, he calls us to something we are wholly incapable of doing. We can't cause someone to be saved; only God can. We can't initiate spiritual growth; only God can. We can't make someone mature or multiply; only God can. The work from beginning to end is God's work, and we are a part of it. Paul understood this: "I planted, Apollos watered, but God gave the growth" (1 Cor. 3:6). Paul knew that just as a farmer puts seed in the ground and waters it, only God can bring new life.

THE WORK FROM BEGINNING TO END IS GOD'S WORK, AND WE ARE A PART OF IT.

Third, this process is relational. Jesus was a relational leader, and the gospel travels along relational lines. Some today think they can advance the gospel solely through impersonal methods. Technology has its place, but it can never replace the personal investment of one's life in another. I saw this most vividly during the recent COVID-19 outbreak. Worship services were broadcast through websites and social media platforms, people flocked to podcasts and eBooks, some groups even gathered on Zoom calls and in chat rooms. And while I am thankful for the technology, I became increasingly convinced that a screen can never replace a touch. Yes, people can grow to a point by listening to podcasts or reading books or watching videos, but each of us needs a person to love us, take us by the hand, and pray for us. We need people to show us an example to follow as they follow Jesus.

Finally, this process is reproducible. Jesus demonstrated how this process was to be done, and he expects us to follow his example. On that mountain, Jesus reminded his disciples of all he had done for them. Now he expected them to do the same. This process is not beyond your ability to follow. Your ministry may be in a rural community or urban center. You may work with young children or recovering drug addicts. It doesn't matter. Jesus' process is simple, powerful, and reproducible.

This simple model of making disciples caused the early church to flourish amid a hostile and pluralistic culture. This simple process fueled great awakenings and turned pagan lands into mission-sending centers. This simple plan even today is the stimulus of growth among underground churches and Christian movements worldwide. Thus, this process is reproducible, and it's not confined to any culture, language, or people group. Jesus gave us his model for the nations, and if you submit yourself to it, you have his promise: "I am with you always, to the end of the age" (Matt. 28:20). Jesus promised his power and his presence. What more could you ask for?

DIVING DEEPER

Now that you have an overview of Jesus' strategic plan, let's do a deeper dive into each of these strategies and how Jesus implemented them in his ministry. In my study of *Harmony of the Gospels*, I discovered that this simple strategy was the precise strategy Jesus employed. If you were to lay out this four-staged strategy across the timeline of Jesus' ministry, you would discover that he followed it perfectly with amazing results. If you are going to follow Jesus' strategic plan for making disciples, you will need to follow it as well.

ENGAGING SPIRITUAL EXPLORERS

After Jesus' baptism, he immediately went into the wilderness to fast and be tempted by Satan. He emerged, filled with the Holy Spirit. He went back to where John the Baptist had been preaching and baptizing. There we read:

> The next day, John was standing with two of his disciples. When he saw Jesus passing by, he said, "Look, the Lamb of God!" The two disciples heard him say this and followed Jesus. When Jesus turned and noticed them following him, he asked them, "What

> are you looking for?" They said to him, "Rabbi" (which means "Teacher"), "where are you staying?" "Come and you'll see," he replied. So they went and saw where he was staying, and they stayed with him that day. (John 1:35–39)

This passage marked the beginning of the explore phase of Jesus' ministry. Jesus interacted with many different people during this phase, inviting them all to "come and see" who he was and what it meant to follow him. After an evening with Jesus, these two disciples were convinced Jesus was the Christ.

One of the disciples, Andrew, went to his brother, Peter, and said, "We have found the Messiah," (John 1:41) and took him to meet Jesus. Then Peter met Jesus face-to-face for the very first time and received a new name. He was no longer called Simon but Cephas ("Peter," which means "rock").

The next day they traveled back up to Galilee where Jesus met Philip. He, along with Peter and Andrew, had grown up in the same small town of Bethsaida. Then Philip, in his excitement, found Nathanael and invited him to meet Jesus. Nathanael asked, "Can anything good come out of Nazareth?" (I see this as typical trash talk between people from two small towns. Trust me, I grew up in one!) To which Philip replied, "Come and see" (John 1:46). Upon encountering Jesus, Nathanael was so overwhelmed by Jesus that he said, "You are the Son of God; you are the King of Israel!" (John 1:49). Those five men were the first to follow Jesus, but they were not the last.

Over the next eighteen months, Jesus took these men on a wild ride. He took them with him to Cana where he turned water into wine, his first miracle (John 2:11). They traveled south to Jerusalem where Jesus turned over the money changers' tables in the temple, encountered the erudite Nicodemus, and returning through Samaria, met a woman at a well. She later ran back to tell her village about Jesus, "Come and see a man who told me everything I ever did!" (John 4:29, NLT). Once back in Galilee, Jesus healed a Roman nobleman's son in Capernaum and was rejected by his own hometown in Nazareth (Luke 4). During this phase, Jesus encountered the religious and irreligious, skeptics and believers, wealthy and poor, powerful and insignificant, the educated and the uneducated, and he invited them all to "come and see."

The first step in Jesus' strategy was to engage people exploring spiritual truth. We live in a culture that is fascinated with spiritual things but ignorant of Jesus and why he came. But they are searching. They are hurting. On the back end of the global pandemic, people are hungry for connection and for help.

Our church is currently planting a church in New York City. The city is known for chewing up church planters and spitting them out! With less than 5 percent of the city's population claiming to know Jesus, it is a field ripe for harvest. But our teams have noticed a change. The isolation and the ubiquitous fear that rested over the city for so long has produced a hunger for community and the answers to life's biggest questions. And this nagging need for hope plagues the minds of both the wealthy and homeless as well as both the Wall Street executive and street-hardened drug dealer because every person has within them the desire to know God.

Jesus was a master at stepping into the pain and questions of the people around him and directing the conversations back to hope. For a church to be successful in this phase, it must have an intentional plan to encounter people with the gospel. What people groups live in the community? What are their needs? What struggles can the church help meet? How can the church engage people in spiritual conversations? What events or initiatives can the church provide to invite the community to "come and see" the beauty of Jesus?

CONNECTING BELIEVERS

After a year and a half, Jesus' ministry was about to take a noticeable turn. Up to this point, John the Baptist had been the public movement leader. His brash, confrontational style of preaching, along with his rugged appearance, made him the quintessential Old Testament prophet, and in reality, he was the last prophet to point people to the Messiah. All prophets before had delivered the message, "He's coming," but John's message was, "He's here!" But soon John was put in prison, and things changed. For a year and a half, John's public ministry had allowed Jesus to move freely under the radar as he drew followers to himself. But now Jesus was about to take center stage, and the curtain would come down on John.

Jesus relocated the base of his ministry from his small town of Nazareth to the thriving city of Capernaum, strategically located along the Via Maris international trade route and along the north shore of the Sea of Galilee. He also began preaching publicly to the crowds the same message of repentance that John had so powerfully spoken. Jesus' disciples had done their best to follow Jesus during the day and fish at night. They still had families to care for and bills to pay. But now Jesus was ready for them to take a significant step in following him.

Matthew 4:18–22 marks this major transition. Jesus walked along the Sea of Galilee, and while seeing Peter and John mending their nets after a night of fishing, he called to them: "Follow me . . . and I will make you fish for people" (Matt. 4:19). Walking down the shore, he gave the same invitation to James and John, the sons of Zebedee. The key phrase, "Follow me," stands out. Yes, Jesus had said those words before, but now they took on new meaning, and Jesus called these men to connect with him in a deeper way: he sought a total life commitment, not part-time followers. And the disciples were ready to make it. Without hesitation, each man walked away from their nets, their livelihoods, and their families to follow Jesus on the expedition of their lives: fishing for people.

Over the next six months they saw the masses healed, a crippled man lowered from a dismantled roof to the feet of Jesus, a miraculous catch of fish, and a leper washed clean. Everything was new, exciting, and unexplainable. The swell of God's power had lifted everyone around them, and history was in the making. During this time, the disciples connected with one another in a deeper way. From this point forward, they would be known as the "Jesus guys," the ones publicly following him.

They also connected with Jesus' ministry in a deeper way. Jesus still did all the work. He taught, healed, and ministered as the disciples shadowed him. But they took it all in because soon Jesus would entrust this ministry into their hands. So Jesus connected these men to himself, to each other, and ultimately to his cause.

Churches that connect believers well are churches that intentionally create pathways for new believers to take the next steps in their faith journey.

They provide easy ways for them to go public in their commitment to follow Jesus. They make it easy to join the church and get into a group. They create on-ramps for new believers to serve and get their hands dirty in ministry and experience God using them in significant ways.

One of the best ways to do this is by serving in the local community. During a Christmas outreach event we hosted for underprivileged kids, a new believer took the risk of joining one of our ministry teams. He was uncertain God could use him in any significant way, but he was available. During the night, a young single mother from the community turned to him for help. She was all alone, raising children with no support and barely making ends meet. Then she asked him, "Would you pray for me?" Fear shot through his body like he had grabbed a live wire, but he steadied himself and said, "Sure." He took her by the hand and prayed for God's care for this young mother. Afterward, he told me with tears streaming down his face, "I can't believe God chose to use me tonight!"

GROWING DISCIPLES

According to Jesus' ministry calendar, he had hit the two-year mark, and it was time to make another significant shift on his leadership team. Luke's Gospel says Jesus spent the night in prayer, asking the Father for guidance, and then chose twelve men to serve as apostles. Up to this point, Jesus had called men to follow him, but now he chose leaders—"apostles"—he would train to lead after he was gone. (The word "apostle" means "sent one.") These were the leaders he would send out to direct the burgeoning Christian movement. These apostles eventually became the established leaders of the movement and the foundation of the early church (Eph. 2:20).

Jesus chose these men to enroll in his school of training. You could label this the "be with me" phase of ministry. For the next six months, Jesus poured all he knew into these men and gave them hands-on experience and teaching. Some of the greatest sermons of Jesus, such as the Sermon on the Mount and the parables of Jesus, are in this section of Scripture. Jesus demonstrated his power over demons, disease, deadly natural forces, and devilish critics, showing himself to be God in human flesh and leaving his disciples to wonder, "What kind of man is this?" (Matt. 8:27). All of this took place as Jesus trained them to follow in his footsteps.

A friend of mine in medical school learned certain surgical procedures by following the adage, "Watch one, do one, teach one." He would *watch* a surgery be performed. Then he would *do* the same procedure under close supervision. Then once he had mastered it, he would *teach* it to someone else. This was exactly Jesus' approach to training. In Luke 8:1, Jesus went throughout the villages ministering as his trainees watched carefully. In Luke 9:2, Jesus sent them to "proclaim the kingdom of God and to heal the sick." And later in Luke 10:1, Jesus sent out seventy-two other disciples in pairs, and while the original twelve apostles are not mentioned directly, they were likely the ones leading these new recruits and teaching them what to do. Watch one, do one, teach one. This growing disciples phase is all about training and equipping, personal investment and accountability, and acquiring the skills and proficiency necessary for multiplication.

Churches that grow disciples well have a clear plan for training up disciple makers and emerging leaders. They have a curriculum that helps them to train up new disciples in the necessary skills for walking with God, reaching their world, and investing in a few. These churches also practice the "watch one, do one, teach one" method of leadership development. They have a proven system to identify emerging leaders and through hands-on training equip them for great levels of leadership and service.

One of the greatest joys in ministry has been the privilege of training people to be disciples and make disciples of Jesus. Doing this gives me a front-row seat to the miracle of God's sanctifying work. This is the joy of ministry. Paul writes to the believers in Thessalonica: "For what is our hope, our joy, or the crown in which we will glory in the presence of our Lord Jesus when he comes? Is it not you? Indeed, you are our glory and joy" (1 Thess. 2:19–20, NIV). Investing in others bears lasting fruit and the joy that comes with it.

MULTIPLYING DISCIPLE MAKERS

The final phase in Jesus' strategy was the multiplication phase. Jesus took his disciples up the far north part of Israel to the town of Caesarea Philippi. Idols saturated the Roman city. Still today you can see the markings of the ancient temples constructed to worship the pagan gods of the day. The centerpiece of it all was a large grotto through which flowed the headwaters of the Jordan River. The people believed this was the gateway to Hades, the underworld. If a sacrifice was thrown into raging waters and it disappeared, then the gods had accepted it. However, if the sacrifice emerged, it was rejected.

This was a very dark place, and Jesus asked his disciples an important question: "Who do people say that I am?" His disciples answered that some said Jesus was John the Baptist come back to life or Elijah or another one of the great prophets. Then Jesus asked, "Who do you say

I am?" Peter, in his boldness, spoke up. "You are the Messiah, the Son of the living God" (Matt. 16:16). Peter had gotten it right. Jesus said Peter's revelation had come from the Father, and then Jesus made this incredible statement: "I also say to you that you are Peter, and on this rock I will build my church, and the gates of Hades will not overpower it" (Matt. 16:18). On the solid foundation of Jesus—the Christ, the Son of the living God—God would build his church. And not even the gates of Hades, not even the dark and pagan world they saw right before their eyes, would stand against it.

Every time I teach this passage standing before the massive grotto, I am struck with the power of Jesus' words. Today, the ancient temples are just a faded memory. They are gone, but the kingdom of Christ is still alive and advancing! Jesus is still building his church. You see, Jesus never told us to build the church. That's his job. Instead, he told us to make disciples, which is our job. And as we make disciples and multiply disciple-making leaders, Jesus builds a church that grows and glorifies him.

For the next nine months, Jesus stressed to his men that apart from sacrifice, spiritual multiplication would not take place (John 12:24). Also during this season the twelve apostles multiplied into seventy-two other disciples who were sent out into the villages of Israel and Perea. And when they returned to report how God had moved and how the demons had been subject to them, we read that Jesus was filled with joy (Luke 10:21). This is one of the only places in the Scriptures where we see Jesus expressly filled with joy. And why was he joyful? Because the movement was multiplying. It had moved now to the fourth generation: from Jesus to his apostles, to the seventy-two disciples, and then to others. Missiologists tell us that when a movement reaches the fourth generation, it cannot be stopped.

In these final months, Jesus continued to declare boldly who he was and why he had come. He said he was the source of "living water" (John 7:37–39); "the light of the world" (John 8:12); "the gate" (John 10:9); and "the good shepherd" (John 10:11) who gives his life for his sheep. He openly revealed his eternality, stating his oneness with the

Father (John 10:30) and his existence before Abraham (John 8:56–58). These statements were met with fierce resistance by the religious elites who, on two occasions, at the Feast of Tabernacles (John 7–8, six months before Jesus' death) and at the Feast of Dedication (John 10, three months before Jesus' death), attempted to kill him. All the while, the gospel went out powerfully, people were changed, and the movement swelled.

To multiply, there must be both the bold proclamation of Jesus and, at the same time, the embrace of self-denial, suffering, and sacrifice that proclamation certainly brings. Jesus understood it, and his disciples would realize it soon enough. This is why we don't see rapidly multiplying movements within the United States today as in other countries around the world. The movements in China, Iraq, and parts of India are perpetuated by disciple-making leaders who boldly proclaim Christ and give no thought to their own safety. All that matters is the preaching of the gospel. All that matters is the hope of bringing Christ to their people.

For example, in Iran the preaching of the gospel remains illegal and comes with the severest of penalties, including prison and death. One pastor, "Wahid," writes, "One day when I went to church, I got a threatening call from the government. After that, I always had a sense of being followed, and my phone tapped. Not an unusual thing in Iran." This pastor ultimately spent time in prison, first in isolation, then in overcrowded all for his faith in Jesus. Wahid recalls, "I often dreamed of getting out of prison, . . . but when I woke up, I realized again that I was still inside."[17] This was the same kind of suffering we saw in the early church and in the ministry of Paul. Yet in their suffering were tremendous joy and hope.

YET IN THEIR SUFFERING WERE TREMENDOUS JOY AND HOPE.

JESUS' PLAN FOR YOU

As you look at Jesus' strategic plan, it is simple. Engage spiritual explorers with the gospel. Connect believers in biblical community and service. Grow disciples by training them to grow in Christ and multiply. And multiply disciple-making leaders who will fuel and exponentially grow the movement—no matter the cost. This simple plan has been the nucleus of every Christian movement on earth. So do you follow it?

Someone once asked the great evangelist Billy Graham if he were the pastor of a church in a large city, then what would be his plan of action. Dr. Graham replied:

> I think one of the first things I would do would be to get a small group of eight or ten or twelve men around me who would meet a few hours a week and pay the price! It would cost them something in time and effort. I would share with them everything I have, over a period of years. Then I would actually have twelve ministers among the laypeople who in turn could take eight or ten or twelve more and teach them. I know one or two churches that are doing that, and it is revolutionizing the church. Christ, I think, set the pattern. He spent most of his time with twelve men. He didn't spend it with a great crowd. In fact, every time he had a great crowd, it seems to me there weren't too many results. The great results, it seems to me, came in this personal interview and in the time he spent with his twelve.[18]

Billy Graham was right. Jesus had a plan, and now he wants us to follow it. Take a long look at your ministry. Put it up against the model of Jesus. How well is your ministry engaging spiritual explorers? How well are you bringing in new believers and connecting them to the church and to the ministry? Are you growing up disciples and training them to walk with God? And to what degree are you multiplying leaders who will fuel the movement? What areas are strong? What needs to change?

As you ponder these questions, let me offer a few very important observations. First, moving through the discipleship pathway requires various levels of movements. Jesus gave his followers opportunities either to step up or step out. For example, exploring the claims of Christ takes little commitment. However, following Jesus and connecting with other believers requires greater commitment. It takes even more commitment to grow and be a part of a group that will train you and hold you accountable. And denying yourself and embracing hardship as you invest your life in others requires the highest level of commitment. With every step, the level of commitment becomes greater.

The second observation is that not everyone is willing to make the commitments necessary to move all the way through the pathway. I wish it wasn't true, but it is. Everything above the diagonal line in our diagram represents the number of people who are willing to take that next step. Many will be willing to at least explore the claims of Christ or hear the gospel message, but fewer will be willing to come to Christ and connect with the church. Even fewer will be willing to grow, and even fewer will be willing to multiply their lives in the lives of others.

Think about Jesus' own ministry. The masses came to hear him speak, but few chose to follow him. We know that after his ascension, 120 people were in the upper room awaiting the Spirit's coming. Jesus had even fewer that he had trained to multiply and lead. The seventy-two others he trained certainly fit in this category. These men went on to multiply, but only a few moved into church leadership, namely the twelve apostles. And even within the twelve, Jesus often invested a disproportionate amount of time with four: Peter, James, John and, at times, Andrew. Therefore, it's true that a greater commitment is at each stage, and not everyone in your church will be willing to make the commitments necessary to multiply. But the ones who will are the leaders to move your ministry forward.

I like to call them the "tip of the spear" because they are your early adapters, your givers, your leaders, your future elders and pastors, your church planters. These are the disciple-making leaders who will shape the future of your ministry and multiply thirty-, sixty-, one hundred-fold and produce fruit that will last until Jesus comes again. You might ask, "If I move people along this disciple-making pathway, how do I move them up into leadership in the church?" That's what you will discover in the chapters ahead.

I began this chapter with the statement: "When you lose your why, you lose your way." We've seen that Jesus offered a very clear "why" for the church. The church exists to make disciples who will multiply into a movement. Jesus not only gave us the "why," but he also gave us the "how." He engineered a pathway perfectly designed to chart a course for people far from God to explore who he is, connect with believers, grow in their faith, and multiply their lives into the lives of others. This was Jesus' plan for his church.

A friend once said, "Jesus started the church the way he wanted it, now he wants it the way he started it." Sadly, many churches seem to have lost their way. You may feel that you have lost your way. Maybe you've drifted from Jesus' priority and his pathway. If that's so, be encouraged. You can take steps to refocus your church and ministry back to the priority of Jesus. And when you do, he will go before you. He will empower you. He will guide you, and ultimately, he will receive all the glory!

Up to this point we've talked about how to make disciples who make disciples in your church, but you may have a lingering question: "How do I take those disciples and turn them into leaders?" And that is what the next chapter is all about.

GROUP DISCUSSION QUESTIONS

1. How have you seen churches drift from Jesus' disciple-making mandate?
2. In which part of Jesus' four-step pathway is your ministry the strongest?
3. In which part of this plan is your ministry the weakest?
4. What hinders people from taking their next steps in their own spiritual journey?
5. What happens to a church that is not balanced in all four phases of Jesus' disciple-making pathway?

DISCIPLE-MAKING MOVEMENT PROFILE

The Ireland Movement

The year was AD 400, and Patricius resided in northeast England. The island had been home to the Britons, the Celtic people who populated what is now the British Isles. However, Patricius's family was Roman, resulting from the Roman occupation of England. He was raised in an aristocratic family, well-educated, and Christian. He was baptized as a youth, educated in the fundamentals of the faith, yet he became quite nominal in his faith. As a teen he loved to ridicule the clergy and run with the wild crowd.

However, his life changed radically when he was captured by Celtic pirates from Ireland and sold into slavery at the age of sixteen. The pirates sold Patricius to a Druid tribal chief named Miliuc moccu Boin, who quickly assigned him to work cattle. During his six years of captivity, Patricius changed. The spoiled young man was now humbled. While working in the fields he observed creation and the glory of God's handiwork. Remembering his Christian upbringing, he now fully devoted himself to Christ. He wrote:

> After I had arrived in Ireland, I found myself pasturing flocks daily and I prayed a number of times each day. More and more the love and fear of God came to me, and faith grew and my spirit was exercised, until I was praying up to a hundred times every day and in the night nearly as often.[19]

He spent the nights with other Briton slaves, many of whom were Christians, who encouraged him in his faith. He came to understand his captors, coming to love them and pray for their salvation. He also learned the language and customs.

One night in a dream, a voice told him to run to the coast: "Your ship is ready." He walked for days and stowed away on a ship headed for England. Back home it was clear that Patricius, or Patrick, was a different person. He trained for the priesthood, immersing himself in Scripture and theology, and he was appointed as a parish priest in England for some time.

Now forty-eight years old, and toward the end of the average life expectancy for that time, Patrick had yet another dream. He had a vision of an angel from God reading a letter from the people of Ireland, begging him to come to them. Recognizing this as his "Macedonian call," Patrick was ordained as a bishop to Ireland and set sail with a team of priests and laymen to evangelize the people.

Ireland was barbarian and uncultured. It was a hostile place. While Patrick's strategy is not overtly recorded for us, by observing his methods, we can understand his predictable pattern. He and a small team approached a village and met with the leaders, seeking to share the gospel with them. They asked permission to set up camp outside the village, and then the team interacted with the people, building relationships, sparking gospel conversations. Members of the team invested more time in those who showed interest by meeting their families and friends. Eventually, new believers were baptized, and a small church began. Then after some time, a few leaders remained with the new church while the rest of the team and a few new converts went to the next village.

This process of relational evangelism, church planting, and leadership development proved to provide a Christian faith that was indigenous to the people and one that could rapidly multiply. Ironically, the religious establishment in England was angry at Patrick for his methods of spending time with such barbarians and sinners. Yet his ministry ignited a movement that transformed the island and provided a hub for missionary work for years to come.

Patrick later wrote:

> This is why it came about in Ireland that people who had no acquaintance with God . . . are recently . . . made a people of the Lord and are known as children of God. . . . For God gave me such grace, that many people through me were reborn to God and afterward confirmed and brought to perfection.[20]

He knew the good work he had done in Ireland was in fact a work of God. Patrick died on March 17, 461, and still today we celebrate his life and impact.

4

THE PIPELINE

The movements of tomorrow depend on the leaders you build today. Most ministry leaders want to build something that matters, something that will last. You probably got into ministry because you had a heart for people or a strong sense of calling. You want your ministry to grow, even to overflow the banks of what is normal or expected, but for that to happen you must raise up leaders. Not just any leaders but multiplying, disciple-making leaders. Remember what we said in the first chapter: your greatest redemptive potential is not measured by what you achieve alone but what can be achieved through you and those you train to multiply! That is how movements begin.

If you follow Jesus, then you are in the movement business. Sweeping, multiplying, God-honoring, culture-changing movements are built as one leader multiplies themself into others who do the same. And that is what Jesus did. Not only was Jesus a master disciple maker but he was also a master movement builder. That his movement still expands and grows all over the world today is evidence of this truth. How did he do it? And how can we follow in his steps? To build a movement, you must make disciples and move them into greater levels of leadership.

THE LEADERSHIP PIPELINE

Over the past twenty years, the term "Leadership Pipeline" has become increasingly common in corporations, both in the United States and around the world. The term originated with the work of Walt Mahler, a human resource consultant, while he worked for General Electric in the 1970s. Mahler's principal work was the discovery of what made emerging leaders successfully rise up through the various layers of an organization. As leaders grew and were promoted from one level of leadership to another, certain new skills, values, and expectations needed to be acquired to remain successful. Each leader had to continue to grow to move up to higher levels of leadership.

As he developed this theory, he was joined by one of his students, Steven Drotter, who continued the research, adding his own discoveries. Sometime later, succession-planning coaches Jim Noel and Ram Charan joined them. Their landmark book, *The Leadership Pipeline*, came out in 2000 and was an overnight success. Many industry-leading companies saw this book as a way for them to keep an edge on their competition. Not too long after, non-profits also saw the benefit of creating a leadership pipeline, which is a strategic plan to identify new leaders, develop them, and move them up through the organization.

Today, churches also adapt these principles to maximize their impact. In the past, churches have relied on bringing leaders in from the outside instead of raising leaders up from within. And the results are mixed. While you might be able to attract highly competent leaders to your ministry who will move the team forward, you also assume a great deal of risk. You don't know that person's character, the health of their family, or how they will interact with your people. Just because they were successful in one ministry context doesn't guarantee they will be successful in your context. And you can't be sure they will buy into your philosophy of ministry.

This is a big one. Probably the greatest mistakes I've made as a leader have been when I brought people into the organization who looked amazing on paper and interviewed well, only to discover later they were never really with me. They brought their ideas of what ministry should look like, but many of those ideas were on a collision course with the direction of our church.

When you look at the early church, you see God raising up leaders from within. These were character-proven, time-tested, doctrinally sound leaders who were elevated into greater positions of influence over time. In Acts 16:1–4 Paul recruited Timothy, likely a convert under Paul's previous ministry in that city, onto his ministry team. Paul had been introduced to Timothy by the leaders of the church in Lystra who knew the young man, knew his family, and could testify to his character and calling. But just because a leader comes from within doesn't guarantee he will be the perfect fit. Barnabas certainly knew John Mark, who joined Paul's ministry team on their first missionary tour, and Mark struggled to meet expectations, eventually abandoning them altogether (Acts 13:13). This caused a significant division between Paul and Barnabas because Paul wasn't willing to risk taking Mark along with the team the second time around (Acts 15:36–39). So bringing up leaders from within isn't foolproof; every addition to the team has its level of risk and reward. Healthy ministries utilize a combination of both.

As we have seen up to this point, Jesus had a very intentional strategy for developing multiplying disciple makers. From the very beginning of his ministry, Jesus engaged these men relationally for the purpose of training them and releasing them into the harvest field. How did he do that? As we discussed in the previous chapter, Jesus recruited men to follow him (Matt. 4:18–19), appointed them to leadership roles (Mark 3:13–14), and released them to raise up more leaders who would grow to become seventy-two (Luke 10:1), 120 (Acts 1:15), and five hundred (1 Cor. 15:6).

JESUS HAD A VERY INTENTIONAL STRATEGY FOR DEVELOPING MULTIPLYING DISCIPLE MAKERS.

Jesus' goal was to release them to lead, multiplying the movement, empowering them by his Spirit. Clearly, Jesus had an intentional strategy for recruiting and developing young leaders who would, in turn, make disciples and lead the church. He constantly filled his leadership pipeline so churches could be planted and the movement could move forward. If

Jesus had a clear plan, then so should we. I'm not suggesting you should never bring a leader onto your ministry team from the outside. But you should weigh the risk, go into it with your eyes wide open, and develop a healthy process of also raising up leaders from within your ministry. And that is what a leadership pipeline will help you do.

Just as you are intentional about moving people *along* the disciple-making pathway so you can multiply disciples, you must also intentionally raise leaders *up* through a leadership pipeline to multiply the movement. And as you will see later in this book, the pathway and the pipeline work together to create multiplying disciples who will multiply a movement.

THREE PRINCIPLES OF A LEADERSHIP PIPELINE

Several years ago, I sat down to read *The Leadership Pipeline*, which is a relatively thick book written for large international corporations. Though the authors intended to write it in layman's terms, it still bears a formal style and employs some technical terms. However, I found the book to be captivating and compelling. I like to scribble in the margins of any book I read, and by the time I had finished it, I had filled it with insights. I quickly transcribed my notes into an executive summary and shared it with our senior leadership team. We then worked with our church staff to improve our system for leadership development. We are still far from where we want to be in this area, but we are making strides. Here are three overarching principles to build your leadership pipeline.

Identify your levels of leadership. The first step to building a leadership pipeline is to identify your existing levels of leadership.[21] It stands to reason that larger organizations will have more levels of leadership than smaller organizations. Google's structure looks much different than that of my favorite doughnut shop down the street. The same is true with churches. Usually, churches begin with a very small leadership structure. When we plant a church, we begin with a team of three, supported by a core team of volunteers. At this level, everyone pitches in to help with everything. The team is tight, and everyone is a generalist. But as the church grows, people who specialize in certain areas are added to the team.

For example, you may hire someone to specialize in worship or guest services or community outreach. You must identify the levels of leadership in your church organization and continue to expand those levels to allow the church to grow. So what are the basic levels of leadership? Here is a simple template that you can adapt to fit your context.

THE LEADERSHIP PIPELINE

The Organization Leader

The Department Leader

The Leader of Leaders

The Team Leader

The Self-Leader

Now let's tackle these one at a time and flesh out the differences.

The first level of leadership is the Self-Leader. This is the person in the organization who doesn't have a responsibility to lead others; they are only responsible to lead themselves. This would be a volunteer in your ministry or someone who serves in your ministry. And as you know, your entire ministry depends on these people. They show up week in and week out to serve the Lord by volunteering their time in his church. This could be a volunteer in your greeting ministry or kid's ministry or someone who helps with the facilities team or counts the offering after the service. Level One is the person whose primary focus is on accomplishing the task assigned to them.

The second level of leadership is the Team Leader. This is the person who has proven their ability to lead themselves and are now ready for the responsibility to lead a team of volunteers and servers. Now when I say a team, I mean a small team, usually between two and fifty people. This could be someone leading a coffee team, teaching a small group, or overseeing a small team of worship leaders. The primary focus of the team leader is helping the team accomplish the work together.

The third level of leadership is the Leader of Leaders. Once a person shows their ability to lead a team well, they may step up to leading the leaders of those teams. This level is often a transitional level in the organization. Self-Leaders and Team Leaders are usually volunteer positions; however, the Leader of Leaders position could move into a part-time or even full-time role, depending on the scope of work and time required. The primary purpose of the leader of leaders is assisting and empowering the team leaders to be most effective. A significant shift now takes place from accomplishing tasks to empowering leaders. This might be a small groups coach who oversees multiple small groups leaders. It might be a men's ministry coordinator who supervises all the different ministry teams of a men's ministry. It might be an usher captain who oversees multiple teams of ushers or greeters. Again, the role is to lead leaders and to make them better, not just to accomplish tasks.

The next level is the Department Leader. This is the leader responsible for an entire department of the church. This could be your students pastor, kids pastor, or worship pastor. This could be your administrator or outreach pastor. This person is responsible for leading an entire department of the church and giving direction to the Leaders of Leaders under their care. The Department Leader always works on the business, not in the business. They think about how to make the ministry grow, how to best manage limited resources, and how to lead a team to accomplish critical goals.

The final level is the Organization Leader. These would include the senior pastor and possibly a senior leadership team or executive team. Some churches employ a board of elders at this level. These people are ultimately responsible for setting vision, executing a strategy, and leading the entire organization toward success. The success of the entire organization ultimately rests on their shoulders. Consequently, these leaders are not only giving oversight to the daily operations and accomplishment of Department Leaders, but they are also looking into the future to identify risks and chart the course for the whole church or organization.

As you look through these levels of leadership, let me make two recommendations. First, think about the terms you want to use to describe each level of leadership. For example, at our church, we use the terms Server, Team Leader, Coordinator, Department Leader, and Senior Leader. Other churches use different names to identify each role. Determining what works best in your context as you name these leaders is important. But then being consistent across the board in using the same titles for every department in the church is equally important. If the kids ministry uses different names from the student ministry or guest services ministry, it will only cause confusion. Keep things simple and keep things consistent.

Second, think about what leadership levels your church currently has and what levels you need to add. As you grow, you will need to reorganize your team so your ministry can continue to expand. When a church just starts, everyone is usually involved in every decision. Staff meetings probably likely include everyone who is receiving a paycheck. But as a church grows, creating new levels of leadership becomes necessary. Specialists can be added to the team. New structures will be required. These transitions can be hard. Some who enjoyed the highest levels of influence may no longer need to be in those places of leadership. This requires honesty, candor, and courage. But these conversations are necessary for a church to continue to grow.

Define the key skills needed to be successful at each level. Each level of the leadership pipeline is vital and unique. Everyone must join together to accomplish the work of the church. That is why you must clarify what it takes to be successful in each leadership role. While large companies create very sophisticated and complicated competency models, I suggest that you start by identifying only the top three to five skills needed to be successful in each leadership role. When we worked through this as a church team, we identified the top five skills or competencies necessary for each level of leadership. Ask yourself: *What is needed for this leader to be successful? What does he need to know? What experiences does she need to have? What coaching will they need from me?*

In the first two levels of leadership (Self-Leaders and Team Leaders) the skills are quite varied. The top five skills necessary for a worship singer are vastly different from the top five skills necessary for a nursery worker. The same goes for the skills needed to lead a team of golf cart drivers and to lead a team of media camera operators. The skills needed in the first two levels of leadership will look very different. However, once you move above that, you will find that the skills needed for the upper levels of leadership look quite similar. This is because the first two levels of leadership are about the performance of tasks, while the top three levels of leadership are all about the performance of leaders. Articulating these necessary skills and competencies is necessary if you want to develop leaders in these skills and help them to grow.

Clarify the commitment required at each level of leadership. As a leader works their way to higher levels of leadership, their commitments (i.e., time and training) will increase. In the first level of leadership, the time commitment will certainly be minimal. Most volunteers or servers commit to a weekly or monthly slice of time and some basic training. Nothing more is expected. But as you move up into leading a team and then leading leaders, your time commitment will increase, as will your commitment to training and development.

In our church we have paid childcare workers on a regular set schedule. They serve at the first level in our organization. If they are required to have overtime, they expect to be paid for it. But we also have a Leader of Leaders who coordinates the teams of paid childcare workers, and she expends a tremendous amount of time preparing for events, training up leaders, managing resources, and ensuring our facility meets and exceeds safety codes. She must be highly trained, and she must be willing to put in the time, even extra hours, to make this a safe and positive experience for our families.

Too often churches assume people know what is expected when it comes to time and training commitments. And those unspoken assumptions are usually the source of conflicts and bad attitudes down the road. Clarifying commitments at each level will serve you well in the long run.

HOW MANY LEADERS DO YOU NEED?

After you have identified your levels of leadership and have written down the skills and commitments necessary for success at each level, you can begin thinking about how many leaders you need. Again, smaller churches may need only ten to twenty leaders in the bottom two levels and only a few in the top levels of the pipeline. Larger churches may need hundreds of leaders at the bottom levels and more in the mid-leadership levels. This process is elastic and should be customized to fit your ministry context. So how many leaders do you need? Answering this question requires a three-step process.

Step 1. Determine what ministry opportunities you have in each ministry department. For example, look at your student ministry department. How many leaders do you need on Sunday morning? How many do you need during the week? Write out all the positions you need filled. Some of them will be level one leaders. You will need people to help set up the room on Sunday mornings or take attendance or greet students at the door when they arrive. You will need level two leaders, such as small group leaders for every age group, discipleship group leaders, prayer group leaders, student worship team leaders. Now write down the level three leaders you need. You may need a small group leaders' coach or a serving leaders' coordinator. Write down all your leadership positions. You should now have a total number of people you need to run your ministry department optimally.

Step 2. Write down the names of the people who are already in those positions. Who are the people you have already trained and equipped for these roles? This is a good time also to consider if you have the right people in the right spots. You may want to think through any anticipated changes that may arise with your existing leaders. Asking questions like *Is this the right person for this role?* and *Will this person be with us over the next year?* will provide you with the information you need to build your team.

Step 3. Determine how many open spots you need to fill to operate at top capacity. These are the new positions you want to fill with new emerging leaders. Once you have a list of positions you need to fill, the people already installed in some positions, and the empty spots you need to develop, you are prepared to go after new leaders to fill those roles. Just remember, the best candidates for leadership roles higher in the organization will be leaders developing well in the lower leadership roles in the organization. You constantly need to ask yourself, *Whom can I develop and move up into higher levels of leadership?* How do you do this? Keep reading.

MOVING PEOPLE THROUGH YOUR PIPELINE

Once you know the positions you need to fill, you can begin building a process of drawing people into your ministry. Again, the reason you do this is so you can expand your ministry's capacity for growth and multiply your church into a movement. In Luke 10:2, Jesus saw the hurting crowd and told his disciples, "The harvest is plentiful, but the laborers are few. Therefore pray earnestly to the Lord of the harvest to send out laborers into his harvest" (ESV). Jesus didn't say, "The harvest is plentiful, but the laborers are few, so I'll just do it myself. Otherwise, it will never get done." But that is what many leaders do. They believe no one wants to help, or no one can do it as well as they can. This is simply not true. If you want more people leading in your ministry, you must pray for God to send them your way, attract them to your ministry, prepare them to be successful, and then release them to do it! In short, you must draw in leaders and develop them at every level.

YOU MUST DRAW IN LEADERS AND DEVELOP THEM AT EVERY LEVEL.

There are four principal steps to moving people up the pipeline. I like to use the acronym RAPS (recruitment, assessment, preparation, support):

Recruitment. This is where you actively recruit potential leaders into your ministry. Jesus was a master recruiter! He built his leadership team by personally recruiting them to follow him (Matt. 4:18–19). In fact, Jesus never recruited the masses; he always recruited individuals. If you want to recruit new leaders well, the best way is face-to-face. The least effective recruitment is an impersonal "all call." This is the slide in worship service, the church newsletter, or the announcement after the sermon. These methods are outdated and simply aren't productive over time. A slightly more effective tool may be recruiting within a small group, but the best recruitment is done one-on-one.

Ask yourself: *How can people apply for a serving role in my ministry area? How can I make it easy for people to let me know they are interested? How will I identify potential leaders? How can I meet face-to-face with potential new recruits?* And if you don't know how to meet new potential volunteers, just ask your existing volunteers who they think would be great at this job. They will most likely surface names you don't even know! Brainstorm with your team for answers to those questions and begin putting solutions into practice. Recruiting is hard and time-consuming. It takes energy and effort. And quite frankly, some leaders don't want to work that hard. But hard work is needed to draw quality leaders into your ministry.

Assessment. After Jesus recruited workers, he assessed their abilities. We know that before Jesus appointed his leadership team, he prayed all night (Luke 6:12). These men had been "shadowing" Jesus for six months, and he had been watching them. I'm not sure what he was looking for in his future leaders. Maybe he was assessing their coachability, watching their attitudes or efforts, or assessing character issues. Before he appointed, he assessed.

Once someone shows an interest in the ministry position, assessing before you appoint is vital. So how do you assess a potential leader?

What characteristics do you look for? What measures will you use to assess their readiness to move to another level of leadership? Some churches rely on spiritual gifts assessments and other types of diagnostic tools. While these have their place (we certainly use tools like this in our ministry):

The best way to assess is to see people interacting in the environment for which you are recruiting them.

This is why I'm a big fan of "shadowing for a day" and apprenticeship programs. Consider asking potential leaders to shadow someone serving in that role on a Sunday morning or midweek environment. Let them get the feel for what it's like to serve in this capacity. Afterward you can debrief them about their experience. This will also give you a great idea of whether this person is a good fit or not. Apprenticeships are another great way to observe people before you place them in a leadership role. Some apprentice systems are designed for level one volunteers. A person may serve as an apprentice under a small group leader before taking on a group of their own. Someone may apprentice as a camera operator or sound board technician before stepping into those roles. Some apprenticeship programs pay college or seminary students a small stipend to serve, and this provides the apprentice ministry experience while exposing the church to potential leader candidates.

Preparation. After Jesus recruited and assessed his leaders, he spent fifteen months preparing them for the work. He spent four times as much time with the Twelve than he did with the crowds. These new leaders were clearly his priority. He didn't throw them into their leadership roles without training them first. Jesus modeled how they should lead. He trained them on the principles of leadership. He allowed them to lead on their own with oversight. And then he released them with his full support.

Now that you have recruited a new leader and assessed their fitness for the role, how will you prepare them for success? This preparation should include skill training. As we mentioned earlier, now that you know what skills are necessary for success in each leadership role, you will need a plan to train them in these skills. Some of this training may require them to read an article or watch a video and discuss it with you or their trainer. Some of this training certainly would involve shadowing someone doing it well. In the lower levels of leadership, this may not be more than a few weeks of skill training. But it is critical to their success and yours.

Please note that this skill training should take place *before* the new leader begins serving in their role. Too often a recruit is thrown into a leadership role without the proper training. This is like throwing someone in the deep end of the pool and hoping they survive, which is a sure way to guarantee turnover and leave a bad impression about ministry altogether. Train them before you place them into their new role. This training should also include spiritual training on how to walk with God, reach their world, and invest in a few. More on this in the chapters to come.

Support. Jesus didn't just leave his disciples to fend for themselves once they were fully trained. He continued to support them through oversight, accountability, encouragement, times of retreat, and prayer. Then after his resurrection, he promised his ever-present Spirit to lead them and help them (John 16:12–15).

As the newly recruited leader serves on the team, how will you support them for the long haul? The best support includes equipping, inspiring, and appreciating your leaders. Let's look at each of these briefly.

THE BEST SUPPORT INCLUDES EQUIPPING, INSPIRING, AND APPRECIATING YOUR LEADERS.

Equipping is the ongoing training you provide your leaders to help them improve and rise to the next level of leadership. Equipping happens best in huddles. At least once a month, level three leaders and above should huddle with their teams to equip them in areas of leadership. This equipping could be reading a book together, watching a leadership video, or discussing a case study. The equipping should focus on the skills they need to be successful in their current role. Remember, the most effective leadership development follows the 70-20-10 rule. Seventy percent of your equipping should be "on the job" training. Twenty percent of your equipping should come from feedback and coaching. And only ten percent should come from formal education or leadership seminars. This isn't to say formal education isn't important, but most of the growth comes from doing the job and receiving feedback. That's why regular huddles, ongoing coaching, and feedback loops are critical for the development of leaders.

If equipping happens best in huddles, inspiring leaders happens best in large groups. These are events where all the leaders of the organization come together for inspirational development and celebration. These large group environments should happen at least twice a year. At our church, we call these Leadership Academy events. We buy lunch and bring in a dynamic speaker to encourage and inspire our leaders for ministry. This is our opportunity to address issues in leadership that would otherwise go underground. We tend to centralize these gatherings around the spiritual and emotional health of a leader, the tactics and effectiveness of a leader, and also the relationships of a leader.

Leadership appreciation is the last element of support. This may be an event you do for all the leaders in the church, or it may be something you do team by team. Either way, it's important to appreciate the volunteer and staff leaders regularly who give so much to make the ministry happen.

WARNINGS

One evening I was headed home from a long day. It was getting dark, and a string of cars was headed toward me on the small two-lane road that runs to my house. I noticed that one car flashed its headlights at me as it passed by to warn me that a police car was up ahead, hunting for speeders. I immediately checked my speed and slowed down. I didn't want to take any chances. Consider this last section as my flashing my headlights in your eyes. This is your warning. Leaders can make some common mistakes when working through leadership development, and like speeding tickets, these mistakes can be very costly. Trust me, I've made them and paid the price. So let me give you four hazards to steer clear of as you go down this road.

Don't promote every person. Just because a person has been successful in one level of leadership doesn't mean they will be successful in the next level of leadership. This is such a common mistake that even high-level executives of international companies make it all the time. For example, a good friend of mine was a highly productive salesman. He was a natural at prospecting new clients, building relationships, and closing the deal. Everyone loved him, and he loved his job. So it made sense when his supervisor asked him to step up to a new level of leadership overseeing a large sales team. Wrong. It was disastrous. He wasn't equipped for the management side of the next leadership level, and his joy and motivation for his job plummeted. He had stepped out of the role he loved and now was in a role he hated. Before long, he asked to move back to his original spot.

Not everyone should be promoted to the next level. Some are simply not gifted in those roles. Before you promote someone, ask yourself the seven C's:

- Does this person have a *calling* to move to the next level?
- Does this person have the *character* to move to the next level?
- Does this person embody the *core values* of the organization?
- Does this person have the *competency* to move up? (You have those skills and competencies written, so this will help you answer this question.)
- Does this person possess the *capacity* to lead at the next level? This is a big one. Some people are stretched to their capacities in their current roles and have no headroom to rise to the next

level of leadership. Some can manage a lot of people, some only a few. Some have high capacities, others low capacities. That's not a negative thing; it's just a reality. Some people are tall, some are short. Neither is right or wrong. Both can be advantageous, depending on the circumstance. Before you elevate someone to a job requiring greater capacity, be sure they have it.

- Does this person have the *commitment* to give? Are they willing to give the time? Are they willing to commit to the training necessary to be successful?
- And last, does this person have *chemistry* with the team? Do they fit? Will they bring out the best in those around them? Don't elevate a person in leadership until you have thought and prayed through these key elements.

Don't allow leaders to skip levels. You may have an incredible leader who looks great. Everyone loves them. They are a star. Allowing that person to skip over the Team Leader role and move straight to being a Leader of Leaders might seem natural. Or it may seem obvious to move that person straight into a Department Leader role, but that would be a mistake. Why? Their development will be shortchanged and stunted because they have not had the experience of leading at all the levels beneath them.

As a young leader, I started serving as a youth intern while attending seminary. Before that I had been a volunteer in my church and even a small group leader. Now as an intern I was starting at the bottom. I set up chairs, cleaned tables, put up equipment, and picked up the pizza. It was grunt work for sure. Then they gave me opportunities to lead teams of students and eventually to train and lead leaders of students. After a year, they gave me a shot at leading the college department, which included managing budgets, recruiting and training volunteers, choosing curriculum, and organizing overseas mission trips. After a while, I moved into an Organization Leader role in the same church, overseeing multiple Department Leaders.

By the time I became a lead pastor, I had developed a body of experience that served me well in my new position. You know how some leaders just know what to do? It's as if they have developed a sixth sense. That leadership instinct is there because over time, through their body of experience, they have cultivated a sense of what to do and what not to do. They have failed enough and succeeded enough to tell the difference. And that body of experience is shortchanged when a person skips a level of leadership. Every leader deserves the privilege of leading at every level because every level has something to teach that they will need to know in the future.

Don't promote someone just because you like them. This is a tough one. Back in the old days, I would meet a person and then instantly want to move them into some level of leadership, just because we hit it off. I'm a positive person by nature. I see the glass half-full most of the time. I believe the best in people. However, this quality has caused me a good deal of grief over the years.

When promoting a person into the next level of leadership, let their past predict their future. In *The Tempest,* William Shakespeare makes the statement, "What's past is prologue."[22] In the play, Antonio uses the phrase to indicate that his past has led him and his friend Sebastian to consider committing murder in the present. The quote is engraved on the National Archives building in Washington, DC. In other words, the behaviors of the past are the best indication of future behaviors. Has this person behaved wisely in the past? Then they will probably do so in the future. Has this person led honorably in the past? Then they will most likely do so in the future. Never allow the personality of a leader to overshadow the past track record. If you do, you may make a mistake you will likely regret.

I remember bringing one young man on the team. He was incredibly talented, likeable, and capable—a people magnet. He was everything we wanted for the position, but I noticed that he had not stayed very long in any one place. After interviewing him several times, we agreed to take a chance on him. However, he didn't last but a few months before he bounced to another organization. His track record was a trend that I chose to ignore, and we paid for it.

Don't allow too many direct reports. I referenced capacity earlier. Everyone has a limited capacity, and a common mistake leaders make is taking a great leader and weighing them down with too many direct reports. A direct report is someone who reports directly to you within the organizational structure of your church or ministry. In Exodus, Moses's father-in-law, Jethro, counseled him to raise up leaders around him to judge and lead the people, and Moses did: "He chose capable men from all Israel and made them leaders of the people, officials over thousands, hundreds, fifties and tens" (Exod. 18:25, NIV). The reason he appointed some over tens, fifties, hundreds, and thousands is because not every person has the same capacity. Moses knew the capacity of his leaders, so he limited their direct reports based on that capacity.

A leader's ability to lead effectively begins to diminish when they are required to manage and develop more than five direct reports. In our church, we had one executive pastor overseeing more than twelve direct reports at one time. It was too much. The whole organization slowed down under the load. Today, five direct reports are the maximum. When the span of care is limited in this way, your leaders will have more emotional and physical energy to devote to the people they lead, and the whole organization will speed up.

The health of your ministry depends on great leaders. You need a pipeline of new leaders whom you can raise up through your ministry so they can grow and thrive. Unfortunately, most churches wait for good leadership to come to them. They hope someone with incredible leadership skills will join their church whom they can place into a prominent role, but that is a risky strategy. Leaders who come from the outside often don't share your organizational DNA or fully embrace your vision. The best strategy is to raise up leaders from within.

THE BEST STRATEGY IS TO RAISE UP LEADERS FROM WITHIN.

How do you do that? We looked at five simple leadership levels for any organization: the Self-Leader, the Team Leader, the Leader of Leaders, the Department Leader, and the Organization Leader. Each one has a unique part to play in your organization. To fill these leadership roles you will need an intentional plan to recruit, assess, prepare, and support leaders at every level.

Perhaps you lead a small upstart ministry, a small church, or a church plant, and you think, *This seems like a structure for a large church. This doesn't apply to me.* Before you dismiss this section entirely, remember your ministry will only grow to the degree that you have great leaders. No leaders, no growth. Many leaders, great growth. Unfortunately, many pastors of small churches fall into the trap of doing everything themselves and ignoring the important work of training and releasing great leaders. Consequently, these pastors burn out and great leaders are left underutilized. The pastor's role is "to equip the saints for the work of ministry" (Eph. 4:12), and this happens best through an intentional leadership pipeline strategy. Maybe you don't need all five levels of leadership right now, but if you grow you will. So plan today with the end in mind. Draft a fully orbed leadership structure and strategy, and then develop it as you grow.

We have looked at the disciple-making pathway of Jesus and the benefits of a robust leadership pipeline. So how do these two concepts work together to produce disciple-making leaders? That is what you are about to discover next. You will see how the pathway and pipeline work together to reveal the preferred trajectory of a disciple-making leader. You will also see how Jesus developed disciple makers and kingdom builders who changed the world.

GROUP DISCUSSION QUESTIONS

1. How would you draw your ministry's leadership pipeline?
2. What parts of your ministry's leadership pipeline need the most work? Why?
3. Describe your process for recruiting and preparing people for new leadership roles.
4. How do you provide support for your leaders throughout the year?
5. What is the most difficult part of developing new leaders?
6. Which of the four warnings mentioned at the end of this chapter resonate with you right now? In what ways have you failed to heed these warnings in the past?

DISCIPLE-MAKING MOVEMENT PROFILE

The Reformation Movement

The Protestant Reformation, a major turning point in church history, was catalyzed by a German Augustinian monk named Martin Luther. The mention of his name conjures up images of a man vigorously hammering ninety-five theses to the door of the church in Wittenberg on October 31, 1517, promoting salvation by faith alone and opposing the Catholic use of indulgences. What may not come to mind when considering Luther is his commitment to discipleship.

We see this commitment lived out in four primary practices. First, Luther's view of discipleship begins centered on a commitment to God's Word. Prior to Luther, men and women sat silently in darkened cathedrals as priests mindlessly read the liturgy to them in Latin. There was little light and little joy, but with the translation of the Scriptures into German, a revival of hope sprang from the Word. The Luther Bible, translated from the original biblical Hebrew and Greek, was published in 1534. Consequently, churches during this period featured raised pulpits to signify the primacy of preaching God's Word. Luther himself declared, "The pulpit is the throne of the Word of God."[23] There could be no true discipleship apart from obedience to God's Word.

Second, Luther personally invested in men. He and his wife, Katharina, often invited friends, students, and guests into their home to gather around the table and discuss the Scriptures. His students were spellbound as he spoke of theology, family, and practical Christian living, writing feverishly his every word. These notes are preserved for us today in *Luther's Table Talks*. This personal investment was important to Luther and demonstrated his commitment to discipling future leaders. Often, these hungry students engaged him for hours, discussing doctrine and practice to the point that Katharina occasionally scolded them for "keeping 'the Doctor' from his dinner."[24] They passed what they learned at his kitchen table on to others.

Luther's commitment to discipleship is also seen in his creation of catechism. Luther saw this as a tool to train up the immature in the basics of Christian doctrine. The pastor's role was to ensure that those under his care were properly discipled in this way. In the preface to Luther's shorter catechism, he warns pastors:

> Oh, you bishops! How will you ever answer to Christ for letting the people carry on so disgracefully and not attending to the duties of your office even for a moment? One can only hope judgment does not strike you! You command the Sacrament in one kind only, insist on the observance of your human ways, and yet are unconcerned whether the people know the Lord's

> Prayer, the Creed, the Ten Commandments, or indeed any of God's Word. Woe, woe to you forever! Therefore dear brothers, for God's sake I beg all of you who are pastors and preachers to devote yourselves sincerely to the duties of your office, that you feel compassion for the people entrusted to your care, and that you help us accordingly to inculcate this catechism in the people, especially the young.[25]

These were strong words from a strong pastor who understood the urgent call to make disciples. Luther knew investing in others was both a duty and a sacred trust.

Catechism was not only a tool for the pastor but also one for the parents who sought to train up their children in the faith. Fellow reformer John Calvin stated:

> If this discipline were in effect today, it would certainly arouse some slothful parents, who carelessly neglect the instruction of their children as a matter of no concern to them; for then they could not overlook it without public disgrace. There would be greater agreement in faith among Christian people, and not so many would go untaught and ignorant; some would not be so rashly carried away with new and strange doctrines; in short, all would have some methodical instruction, so to speak, in Christian doctrine.[26]

Luther led by example in this way. Many paintings are of Luther sitting in his home and playing the guitar with his family gathered at his feet. This depicted his own priority of family worship and devotions.

Last, Luther's commitment to discipleship is seen in his efforts to train pastors. Luther not only taught theology at the University of Erfurt, but many universities were established due to his influence. These universities sought to train pastors and leaders to lead their churches as disciple makers from the pulpit, in their homes, and with their families. These leaders were how Luther's influence continues to spread even today.

Luther's emphasis on disciple making is what fueled the Reformation. His strong and high view of Scriptures, his passionate investment in the men of his church, his call to parents to disciple their children, and his training of pastors at the university became the core tenets of the movement that shook Europe and the world.

5

THE TRAJECTORY

Jesus was a disciple maker and a movement builder. He was able to do both at the same time. To the casual observer, Jesus might have appeared not to do much. Some think Jesus just went from village to village preaching and performing miracles with little thought of developing his leaders. However, when you dive deeper, you find that Jesus was very intentional in his actions. He was intentional to develop men who could make disciples after he was gone. He was also intentional to develop leaders to lead the movement.

For your ministry to be healthy, you must accomplish both things simultaneously. You must fixate your thoughts on both making disciples who can multiply and developing leaders who can multiply a movement. It's slow work. Arduous and painstaking at times. There is no quick fix. Even after Jesus had worked consistently for over three years, he still had only 120 leaders in an upper room waiting for the Spirit to come. In modern terms, that doesn't look like success. However, those 120 leaders—because they were disciple-making leaders who had been trained and prepared—were the ones to ignite a movement that quickly swept the world.

Most churches fixate on the platform more than they do people. Most are enamored with the personality of the key leader or the worship experience more than working on an intentional process for making disciples and developing qualified leaders to grow the movement. So how do you do both? What does it look like to make disciples *and* develop disciple-making leaders? This is where the pathway and the pipeline come together.

Up to this point I have focused on two important aspects of leadership development. First, I introduced the disciple-making pathway and how Jesus moved his men down this pathway to develop them spiritually. Next, I unpacked the leadership pipeline where we looked at the five leadership levels and how to recruit and develop leaders at every level. Now I want to use this chapter to describe how the pathway and the pipeline work together to produce disciple-making leaders within your church. Then for the rest of the book, I will take a deeper dive into each level of leadership, and we will see how Jesus developed his leaders in those stages.

THE DISCIPLE-MAKING PATHWAY

In Chapter 2 I discussed the church's priority, which is to make disciples. In Chapter 3 we looked at Jesus' fourfold process of making disciples, which was engaging spiritual explorers, connecting new believers, growing disciples through personal investment, and multiplying disciples who make disciples to the ends of the earth.

THE DISCIPLE-MAKING PATHWAY

Explore — Connect — Grow — Multiply

My passion over the past twenty-five years of ministry has been to lead our church to follow Jesus' model. It hasn't been easy work, but it has been incredibly rewarding. Over the years, I've discovered some reasons that following Jesus' pathway is the best way to lead your church and fulfill your ministry.

First, this pathway focuses your ministry on the priority of making disciples who make disciples. As I speak to church leaders across the country, most do not have a clear definition of a disciple. They are not sure if they have made any disciples, and many would be hard-pressed to point out any disciples who have reproduced. It is sad, but true. Most churches just seem to run programs and offer worship services, hoping disciples will be made. We can do better. Following this pathway allows you to be extremely intentional in setting the direction of your church and measuring the effectiveness of your ministry.

Second, this pathway aligns your programming. A friend once conducted a survey of hundred churches and asked them to label their programming along the disciple-making pathway. They categorized their programming based on whether it was engaging spiritual explorers, connecting believers, growing disciples, or multiplying disciple makers. Once the data was in, the results were shocking. According to the survey, 87 percent of the churches had all their programming in the "connecting believers" stage. All of it. That means no programming had been created for engaging spiritual explorers or growing disciples or multiplying disciple makers. All their programming was designed to connect believers. Only this kind of programming results in an anemic and stagnant church. But following the disciple-making pathway allows you to evaluate your ministry and bring health and balance. You can quickly diagnose areas that are weak in your ministry and add programming wherever needed.

Also, the pathway naturally deepens your ministry foundation. As more people move down the pathway, more people connect in community, serve, grow in their walk with God, share their faith, invest in others, and multiply the ministry. All of this deepens your church's spiritual life and strength. The whole attitude of the church begins to mature. A common language develops. A collective understanding of what the church's role is forms. A unity around the mission strengthens. The church is less likely to get in squabbles about ministry philosophy or peripheral matters.

Every time you move a person down the pathway, it's like driving piers down under the foundation of your home. It adds strength and stability, and a stable foundation is required if you are going to build upon it. This reminds me of Jesus' illustration at the end of his Sermon on the Mount:

> Therefore, everyone who hears these words of mine and acts on them will be like a wise man who built his house on the rock. The rain fell, the rivers rose, and the winds blew and pounded that house. Yet it didn't collapse, because its foundation was on the rock. (Matt. 7:24–25)

Granted, Jesus was speaking about obedience to the kingdom principles he had just taught, yet when you consider that this sermon was preached just after he had appointed the Twelve and before their leadership training, clearly Jesus believed his training and preparation of these men would eventually produce a solid foundation upon which to build a movement. The same is true for your church. The more you move people down the pathway, the more you build a solid foundation for your church.

This leads to my last point: following Jesus' pathway results in multiplication. Can you point to an area of your church that is currently multiplying? Is there any area of your church where leaders are reproducing leaders? Where are disciples reproducing more disciples? If you want to see multiplication, then you must prepare people to multiply. And the best way to accomplish this is by following Jesus' disciple-making pathway.

Part of our church code states, "We don't maintain; we multiply." It's more than a catchy statement. It's a mandate. It's an expectation. We expect disciples to multiply by making disciples. We expect groups to multiply by launching new groups. We expect our church to multiply by planting other disciple-making churches, both in the states and around the world. Why?

Because without multiplication there is no movement, and Jesus came to build a movement.

THE LEADERSHIP PIPELINE

In the previous chapter, I gave you a simple overview of the leadership pipeline, which is a strategic plan to identify new leaders, develop them, and move them up through the organization. And this is critical to the ministry of your church. Without new leaders, you are stuck. Without new leaders, you can never multiply. If every person has a given capacity, then there is a certain capacity for your existing leadership team, and they cannot move past that capacity to new levels of growth without new leaders. You must raise up new leaders, and the best way to do that is through a leadership pipeline. This pipeline identifies at least five levels of leadership: the Self-Leader, the Team Leader, the Leader of Leaders, the Department Leader, and the Organization Leader.

THE LEADERSHIP PIPELINE

The Organization Leader

The Department Leader

The Leader of Leaders

The Team Leader

The Self-Leader

Developing this pipeline is essential for your church and ministry growth. After all, if you need more leaders to grow, then somehow you must develop them. And if you are going to develop new leaders, then you need a plan. And that is where most ministries fail—they have no clear process for developing leaders. This is why the pipeline is so important, and this is why our church works hard to implement it across the board.

Whereas the pathway focuses your ministry on the priority of making disciples, the pipeline focuses your leaders on developing new leaders. Without some clear process, few leaders seek to raise up leaders. In fact, it's quite the opposite. Many leaders see the emergence of new leaders as a threat to their own positions and therefore resist developing leaders. They think, *Well, if I raise up someone who can do my job, then what will I do?* This kind of small thinking keeps the overall ministry small.

Just as the pathway aligns your programming, the pipeline aligns your departments because now every department has the same structure, the same recruiting protocols, the same assessment process, the same preparation strategies, and the same support tools for new leaders. This commonality brings clarity and unity to your team. The opposite course would be to allow each department to do their own thing, resulting in confusion and chaos. With a strong leadership pipeline, you now can expand your ministries, grow new groups, and launch new initiatives because you have the leaders to do it.

YOU NEED A WAY TO RAISE UP LEADERS WHO WILL DO THE WORK.

And the result is a movement. Think about how God could use your church to infiltrate your community! Think about how God could use your church to show his compassion to the poor, to plant new churches, or expand his kingdom around the world. All of this is possible, but you need a plan. You need a way to raise up leaders who will do the work.

SYNERGY

We see synergy in many ways. In business, often companies will forge a partnership or merger because they are stronger together than they are independently. For example, in Suzanne Collins's *The Hunger Games,* Katniss Everdeen and Peeta Mellark work together to survive the Hunger Games challenge and take on the autocratic, evil regime of the Capitol. Their combined efforts create synergy. The same is true with making disciples and developing leaders—the pathway and the pipeline work together to create synergy, resulting in a disciple-making leader. Jesus understood this. He moved people along the pathway but simultaneously elevated leadership up the pipeline. He knew disciple making and movement building had to be done together.

So how do the pathway and the pipeline work together to produce disciple-making leaders?

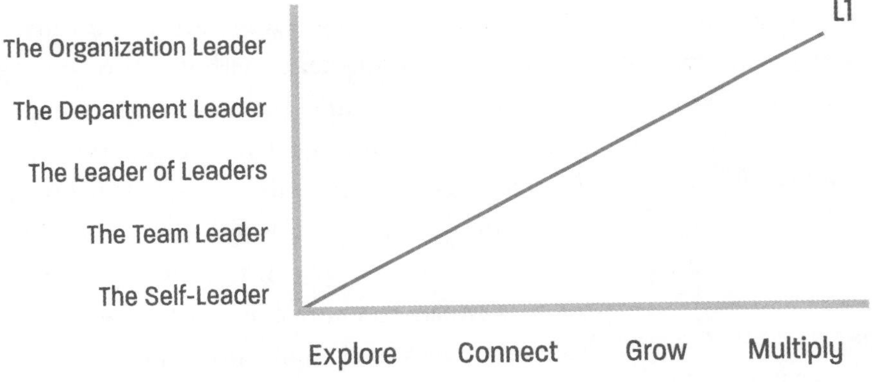

Optimally, a person should move along the disciple-making pathway. As they advance as a disciple, only then can they elevate into leadership. For example, a person may be in the explore stage of their spiritual journey. They ask spiritual questions, wrestle with the claims of Christ, and find the church to be a safe place to grow. Even in this stage, a person can serve or volunteer. They will not qualify to serve in teaching roles or places of spiritual leadership, but they can be a greeter or help on the café team or take attendance in a group. In fact, many people find serving to be one of the best ways to connect to God's people in this stage of their development. As they come to Christ and get involved in group life, they can continue to serve. This person can even serve as a Team Leader in certain aspects of the church. They might lead a team of sound technicians or a crew that upkeeps the facility. As they mature in God's Word, they can even be a small group leader or serve in students or kids ministries. At this point they grow tremendously and see how God uses them to impact others.

Then they take the next step in their spiritual journey. In this environment they learn how to walk with God on their own, deepen their prayer life, read the Bible for themselves, and memorize Scriptures. They learn how to stand against temptation, walk in personal holiness, and celebrate God's grace. They learn how to share their faith and how to invest their life in another person. And if they exhibit leadership capabilities while being discipled, they may rise to be a Leader of Leaders. They may become a small group coach or a greeter captain, coordinate the women's ministry, or oversee a missions team with its various ministries. After some time, they now begin to multiply themself into the lives of others. They disciple a group of men or women. This leader exemplifies maturity and godliness, and they may experience a clear call to ministry. As this call is clarified and corroborated by the church body, they may even move up to be a Department Leader or Organization Leader. This is the optimal trajectory to leadership. One elevates into leadership only to the degree that they progress along the pathway.

ONE ELEVATES INTO LEADERSHIP ONLY TO THE DEGREE THAT THEY PROGRESS ALONG THE PATHWAY.

AN EXAMPLE OF THE PREFERRED TRAJECTORY

This was the exact pathway Zach took. He had come to Christ as a teenager and was faithfully involved in ministry growing up. After college, he married his high school sweetheart and launched into his career. When they joined our church, life was busy. They had little kids at home, and Zach was climbing the corporate ladder. They immediately connected in a group and found community with great friends in their same stage of life.

One day, a pastor from our church invited Zach to be part of his disciple-making group. That is where things began to change for Zach. He started growing in his walk with Jesus. God's Word came alive to him. He was passionate about his faith and living on mission. At the same time, Zach began taking on more responsibilities in ministry. First, he served as a volunteer, and then he began to lead teams. He served as a Leader of Leaders, coaching several small group leaders for a period. Zach grew spiritually, and he grew in his leadership simultaneously.

Sometime later, the person who discipled Zach invited him to go to Zambia to help disciple leaders in that country. On another occasion, they went to Israel, and Zach began meeting passionate disciple makers serving God all over the world. Soon Zach felt a strong call to leave the corporate world and invest his life in ministry. This was a difficult decision. It meant leaving the company where he was so successful and taking a cut in pay, but the Lord had made it crystal clear.

So Zach stepped away from his role and came on the staff as a Department Leader who led disciple-making groups. His business background was immediately felt on the team. He was a gifted leader. A few years later, Zach was asked to serve as pastor of operations on our senior leadership team. Today he serves in that capacity and has a passionate call to make disciples and help lead a disciple-making church.

As Zach journeyed along the pathway, he was elevated up the pipeline to greater leadership roles according to his gifting. This is where you see the synergy of the pathway and the pipeline coming together. As Zach grew as a disciple and then a disciple maker, he was simultaneously elevated into higher levels of leadership. This pattern of development guarantees that you make disciple-making leaders, and disciple-making leaders are critical to church health. They lead from the clear passion and understanding that the church exists to make disciples and multiply. And they lead with a proven track record of spiritual growth that sets an example for others to follow.

This preferred leadership trajectory (L1) is healthy, even if this person never elevates up the leadership pipeline. As mentioned before, not everyone should move up the leadership pipeline. Some are tremendous people and authentic disciple makers but are not gifted, called, or have the character or capacity to lead. However, even if this person only elevates to the point of leading a team or leading leaders, this person is still a mature disciple maker, leading out of the overflow of that spiritual maturity. In this case, every person in leadership is a disciple-making leader. Everyone in leadership sets an example for others to follow. This should be the norm. Write this down and make it a rule: never move someone up into leadership who has not first moved down the disciple-making pathway.

DIVERGENT PATHS

Two examples of leadership don't follow this pattern and cause the church to struggle.

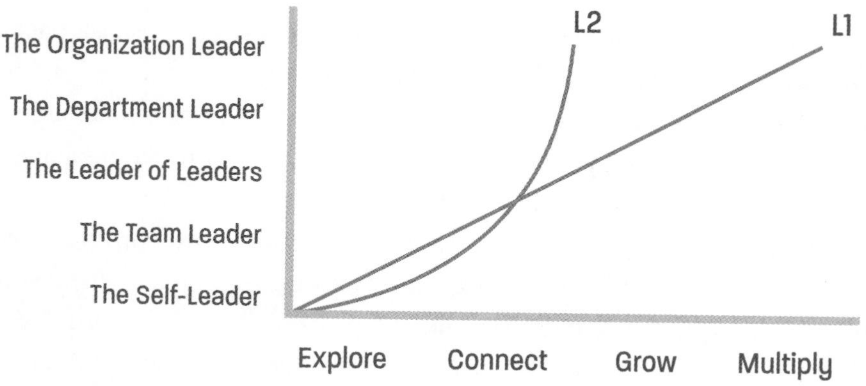

The leader who is not a disciple maker. This is the person who comes to Christ or was maybe raised in the church. He feels a call to ministry, so he goes to a Bible college. There he learns God's Word and begins preaching on the weekends or for special youth events. After college he goes straight to seminary where he gets a master's in biblical studies. A church quickly calls him to serve on their staff as a youth pastor. Soon he moves to a larger church, and then to an even larger church. At some point along his career path, he becomes a senior pastor where he has leadership over an entire church.

At every step along the way he proves to be a smart leader, strategic thinker, great Bible preacher, and compassionate shepherd, but he is not a disciple maker. His leadership trajectory is depicted (L2) on the graph above. You can see he quickly elevated to higher and higher levels of leadership, but he never progressed down the disciple-making pathway. No one ever personally discipled him.

Unfortunately, this is the leadership pattern of most in ministry today. The ramifications of this kind of leadership are devastating. For one, because this person has never truly been discipled, he is in grave danger of using the ministry as a surrogate for his own personal walk with God. Soon sermon preparation is his main time in God's Word. The functional aspects of serving the Lord eclipse his pursuit of Jesus and the health of his own soul. Doing supersedes being. Leadership status replaces spiritual maturity. His relationship with Jesus is understood in terms of what he does for Jesus. Most of the pastors today who struggle with depression, burnout, or hidden sin issues have done so because the demands of ministry strangled their personal walk with God. This is incredibly dangerous for the leader, his spiritual health, and his sustainability.

Another great danger is that this pastor struggles to lead by example. Because he has not been personally discipled and has not developed some of the core disciplines of walking with God, reaching his world, or investing in a few, he becomes increasingly dependent on programs to lead the church spiritually instead of his own personal investment. Consequently, his primary focus becomes gaining weekend worship attendance, baptisms, and giving, and not the overarching goal of making disciples who will reproduce. He is then susceptible to the "superstar" mentality that was mentioned in the first chapter.

If the church's success derives from the leader's charisma, creativity, and personality, then he will be reluctant to raise up other leaders around him who might rival those skills. Therefore, instead of raising up disciple-making leaders, he resists people moving up through the leadership pipeline. This kind of leader causes the ministry to suffer. He is, in effect, holding the church back from all it could be because of his resistance to multiplication.

As you read this, you may see that this L2 leadership trajectory is like your own. You rose quickly through the ranks of leadership, but you never were personally discipled, nor do you have a passion to make disciples who multiply. What should you do?

Let me share an example of Josh, who joined our team from a growing church in our area. He was a charismatic leader with a super likable personality. He played college football and possessed a natural confidence that drew people to him. He had come to Christ as a young boy. His father was a senior leader in multiple churches. After college he sensed God's call to vocational ministry and threw himself into every opportunity to serve the Lord. He married and moved to New York to be a coach and teacher at a small Christian school in Long Island. Later he moved to Texas, serving in various churches as a youth pastor and next generation pastor.

He joined our team as our pastor of community engagement. In this role, he led three Department Leaders. However, by his own admission, he had never been personally discipled. Of course, people in his life had made a lasting impression. His parents had much to do with his spiritual formation and continued to make a lasting impact on him. Other coaches, teachers, pastors, and mentors contributed to his spiritual growth, but no one discipled him in a way that showed him how to disciple others. Josh was an L2 leader.

During his first year on our team, he was part of a Grow Group that challenged him to take his next steps down the disciple-making pathway. He jumped in wholeheartedly with the same exuberance and zeal that had made him successful in so many areas of his life. As Josh began to grow and be stretched, he began understanding Jesus' vision for making disciples who multiply. He started investing in other leaders and raising up people behind him. Now men in our church leadership are a part of his spiritual family tree.

Over time, Josh moved from just being a superstar leader to becoming a fruitful and passionate disciple-making leader multiplying his life for the cause of Christ. He is the kind of leader we want our people to emulate. Hebrews 13:7 says, "Remember your leaders, who spoke the word of God to you. Consider the outcome of their way of life and imitate their faith." Josh is an example our leaders can follow.

If your story is like Josh's, follow his example. Josh humbled himself and submitted to the disciple-making process. Some leaders may instinctively know they need someone to invest in them, but because they are already in positions of leadership, their pride gets in the way and prevents them from growing. They might say, "I already know all of this," or, "This is too basic for me." This merely masks the need for growth in their lives. Some feel if they admit they have never been discipled, people will lose respect for them. But that is not the case. Josh embraced humility and acknowledged he had room to grow. Rather than losing respect from his peers, he gained respect. He showed he was a learner who strove to walk with God in deeper and deeper ways.

Next, embrace accountability, just as Josh did. He started memorizing Scripture. Not reluctantly but with eagerness. He started journaling for the first time in a long time. He started learning a new tool to share his faith and start spiritual conversations. He had the attitude of a learner, which is the definition of a disciple. Embrace investment. Humbly and eagerly step into relationships that will challenge you to be all you can be in Christ.

And last, enthusiastically share what you know with others. Josh couldn't wait to disciple his first group of men. And when he did, it was like getting a front-row seat to life change. He saw men come alive spiritually. He saw the fruit of his investment, which changed him for good. If you will do these things, you can move the trajectory of your leadership from L2 to L1. You will become a disciple-making leader who passionately leads the church to live like Jesus.

The disciple maker who is not a leader. This is the second example of leadership that is dangerous. This is the leader who moves along the disciple-making path, even to the point of multiplying other disciple makers, but never rises to leadership. This person could be an L3 leader but doesn't achieve it fully. This person joyfully makes their way down the disciple-making pathway for exploring the claims of Christ and coming to faith in Jesus. They connect with the church and begin serving in simple ways. Because of their desire to grow, they quickly move into a disciple-making relationship and begin maturing in their faith. Before long, they are making disciples, but they never rise up the leadership pipeline. Sometimes this happens because they are not gifted or called to higher levels of leadership, or a superstar leader over them never gives them the opportunity.

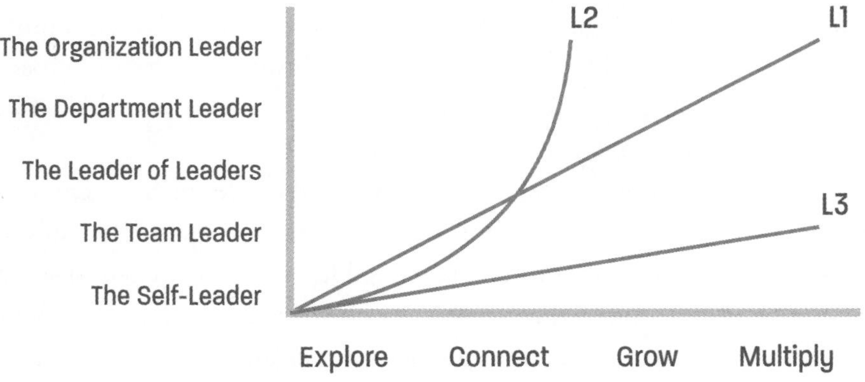

But there is another reason these qualified people don't take on greater leadership roles. Some are more concerned with their own personal discipleship ministry outside the church than they are the overall ministry of the church. Often these people feel the typical church in America is too weighed down with programs and structure to the point that the leader believes their best investment of time and energy is in their own individual ministry. They have lost the value of the body of Christ working together toward a common goal.

A friend of mine was trained for many years by some of the best disciple makers in the nation. He knew the Word and actively shared his faith and discipled men, but his relationship with the church was somewhat distant. Whenever he was invited up into leadership, he declined. When I probed deeper, he said he had limited time balancing a busy career and family and that his best investment was in his personal discipleship ministry outside the church. My friend is an incredible leader, but he chose to opt out of using that gift in the church.

Maybe that is you. Maybe you have honed your disciple-making skills, yet you see leadership in the church as a poor use of your time and resources. If so, let me just remind you that ministry has never been a solo activity. Jesus' own ministry was to establish the foundation of his church as he prepared the leaders who would eventually structure and lead the early church (Matt. 16:18; Eph. 2:20). From the very beginning, the work of the church was a coordinated work. All the gifts of the Spirit are to build up the body and contribute to the common cause of making disciples (Eph. 4:12; 1 Cor. 12). Don't rob the church of your gifting. If God brought people to invest in you and show you how to make disciples, then wouldn't he want his whole church to be filled with men and women like that? Maybe the people in your church are not committed to disciple making because no one has invested in them. Plenty of hungry people are within the walls of the church and long for someone to invest in them. They pray for it, and you just may be the answer to those prayers. Your investing in people in the church could change the whole course of the church.

DON'T ROB THE CHURCH OF YOUR GIFTING.

A friend of mine named Jerry had his own construction business. As a young college student, he was discipled by a pastor who was on fire for Jesus. Throughout his career, Jerry consistently and intentionally made disciples. However, not everyone welcomed his investment. At one point, even the pastor of his home church became resistant to Jerry's investment in other men in the church. At that time, home groups were looked down on, and the pastor feared losing control of his congregation. Jerry could have pulled away from the church at that time and no one would have blamed him, but he didn't. He continued to stay involved, and he continued to lead under the blessing and direction of his pastor and continued to disciple men with his pastor's blessing. Over several decades, Jerry's influence completely transformed this church. It became a church fervent in prayer, generous in giving, compassionate to its community, and diligent in making disciples of all nations.

If you withhold your leadership gifts from the church, then you may hinder what God wants to do through you to bring health and vitality back to his church. If you are an L3 leader and you are invited into places of leadership within your church, say yes. You don't need to force yourself into leadership roles. Those invitations will come to you. And when they come, see them as God-given opportunities for you to broaden your influence and champion the cause of disciple making within your church. The church needs more men and women like you.

Jesus is our model. He was committed to making disciples and building a movement. And his church today needs to recover both goals. I hope by now you are beginning to see how the pathway and the pipeline work together to do that. By creating a culture in your church that utilizes Jesus' disciple-making pathway, you will make and multiply disciples. And by building a leadership pipeline that intentionally raises up leaders throughout your ministry, you will expand your influence and fan into flame the movement of Jesus.

But still many questions are unanswered. How did Jesus raise up leaders as they progressed along the pathway? What did he teach them? How did he warn them? What specific skills did he train them in at each stage of their development? The rest of this book will answer those questions. We will look at every step along the pathway and how Jesus trained his men and then gradually elevated them into positions of leadership. Along the way we will look at modern research on the keys to success at each leadership level. By the end, we will have the tools we need to make disciples and build leaders.

GROUP DISCUSSION QUESTIONS

1. What is your reaction to the statement "Jesus was a disciple maker and a movement builder"?
2. What questions came to your mind as you saw the leadership pipeline combined with the disciple-making pathway?
3. What dangers come with raising leadership up the pipeline before they progress along the pathway?
4. What keeps a disciple-making person from rising up the leadership pipeline?
5. How would you assess your ministry leadership right now? Are they disciple-making leaders? Are some in leadership positions who are not proven disciple-makers?
6. What are some next steps for your ministry as you evaluate this chapter?

DISCIPLE-MAKING MOVEMENT PROFILE

The Awakening Movement

Give me one hundred men who fear nothing but sin and desire nothing but God, and I care not whether they be clergyman or laymen, they alone will shake the gates of hell and set up the kingdom of heaven upon the earth.

— John Wesley

The Church of England at the time of John Wesley's life and ministry was a field of dry bones, lifeless and disconnected from the global commission of Jesus. This is the world John Wesley grew up in. Coming from a long line of pastors and theologians, John showed a special acumen toward matters of ministry, and under the tutelage of his mother, Susanna, he developed a hunger to follow in his father's footsteps. It wasn't, however, until after a failed ministry in the colonies that John returned home and had an encounter with God at the church of Aldersgate, where he found his heart strangely warmed, and he came to know Jesus in a life-changing way. This transformational event fueled Wesley to lead a revival that transformed England and beyond. What was his strategy?

First, John was compelled to take the gospel to those who needed it most. While most churches denied Wesley and his colleague, George Whitefield, access to their pulpits, both men chose to take their preaching to the common people, men and women who would never darken the door of a church. His preaching drew great crowds, and many came to faith in Jesus. This open-air preaching was controversial, and most of the established church leaders condemned the practice.

John most clearly saw resistance when he returned to his home church in Epworth, where his father had pastored, only to be denied the pulpit. Crowds had come, restless to hear Wesley. An announcement was made that Wesley would speak at six that evening, not in his father's pulpit but standing outside on his father's tombstone. Hundreds gathered to hear his gospel message, and many came to Christ. Wesley, later reflecting on that moment, wrote, "I am well assured that I did far more good to my Lincolnshire parishioners by preaching three days on my father's tomb than I did by preaching three years in his pulpit." Basil Miler, in his biography on Wesley, states, "Wesley's voice was drowned by the cries of those seeking salvation. The last meeting continued for three hours, so tender the touch of heaven and the ties of friendship."[27]

Second, Wesley gathered new believers into societies, that is, larger worship services, for the express purpose of biblical teaching, public reading of Scripture, worship, and prayer. John and his brother Charles led these societies until the movement grew too large and required emerging leaders. While the societies proved beneficial to help these believers grow in their faith, they soon were too large to facilitate personal accountability.

Wesley later developed a third priority: the formation of classes, which were mixed groups of men and women, ten to twelve in number, created to facilitate spiritual growth and accountability. The classes also transformed the English working class because careful attention was made to mix people from various socioeconomic stages in these classes to provide mutual respect and unity around the gospel. Leaders of these classes spoke openly and honestly about their failures, and mutual encouragement toward spiritual growth was a priority.

The final piece to the Wesleyan strategy was the creation of bands. These bands, unlike the classes, were strictly gender specific and focused on deeper spiritual development. From these bands Wesley drew mature leaders to multiply the movement.[28] Wesley empowered common men and women, who were without a proper education or credentials, to preach and lead. This was a radical practice in his day and vehemently opposed by the religious establishment.

Wesley was a powerful evangelist. Thousands came to hear him preach, but the genius of Wesley wasn't his preaching; rather, it was his ability to organize societies, classes, and bands that proved effective in raising up leaders and establishing disciple-making communities across the nation. As George Whitefield later confessed: "My brother Wesley acted wisely. The souls that were awakened under his ministry he joined in societies, and thus preserved the fruit of his labor. This I neglected, and my people are a rope of sand."[29] Wesley did not leave a "rope of sand" behind, but rather a multiplying army of disciple-making leaders who singlehandedly transformed Britain and fueled a worldwide disciple-making movement.

PART 2

MULTIPLYING THE DISCIPLE-MAKING LEADER

6

DEVELOPING SELF-LEADERS

Before you can successfully lead others, you must first prove to be able to lead yourself. How can you lead others to manage time if you don't manage your own time? How can you lead others to take initiative if you don't take initiative? How can you lead a team to accomplish goals if you don't accomplish your own goals? Without self-leadership you cannot set an example for others to follow, and you cannot call people to a higher standard. You simply personify the old mantra, "Do as I say, not as I do." That is not leadership at all. Leadership begins with leading yourself. This is how Jesus led his men.

Jesus' leadership style was consistently and passionately calling others to follow him. Jesus set the example for others to follow. In Mark 10:32 we read, "They were on their way up to Jerusalem, with Jesus leading the way" (NIV). This verse has always stood out to me. They all traveled along the road, but Jesus led the way. He was out front setting the pace. Thus, Jesus led the way by setting an example in every aspect of life and ministry. This is the essence of genuine leadership. No one wants to follow a person who doesn't embody the values or exhibit the behaviors they expect in others. We all want to follow someone who leads the way just a few steps ahead of us. That is what Jesus did. And this is where leadership starts: leading yourself before you lead others.

THE IMPORTANCE OF SELF-LEADERS

Self-Leaders are the bedrock of every ministry. From an organizational standpoint, Self-Leaders are those who serve or volunteer in your ministry. They are not asked to lead others; they are only asked to lead themselves and to accomplish a specific task. This category makes up most of the workers in every church or ministry. Without volunteers, nothing would get done. Without Self-Leaders, the ministry would come grinding to a halt.

> **SELF-LEADERS ARE THE BEDROCK OF EVERY MINISTRY.**

Think of the cashier at the grocery s, Chaptetore. Although they may be the least paid and have the least training, they are in contact with hundreds of customers every single day who flow through their checkout area. Now think of a waitress at a restaurant, a receptionist at a doctor's office, a mechanic at a car shop—each is a hands-on worker at the entry level of an organization with direct contact with customers. These are the Self-Leaders.

From a ministry standpoint, they are the greeters, the coffee team members, the baby rockers, the attendance takers, the social planners, the offering counters, the camera operators, the special events hosts. They are the army of workers who move the ministry forward. These Self-Leaders are seldom recognized, often serve behind the scenes, and give their time and talents willingly without payment. They are the people who get the work done; consequently, they are the first to have direct contact with people. That is why these people soon become the face of your ministry and can leave either a positive or negative impression on guests and members alike.

Ironically, this group is often overlooked when it comes to training and development. Most ministry leaders simply tell the person what to do, then leave them to do it with little thought of what it might look like to develop this person beyond their current serving role. In many ways the Self-Leader strata of the organization is a gold mine of future potential leaders with deployable talents and skills who can rise through the leadership ranks. So you don't want to ignore them or look past them. You want to develop them.

WHAT DO SELF-LEADERS NEED?

What do Self-Leaders need to be successful in their important roles? Here are a few things to consider.

First, these self-leading volunteers need clarity and training on their specific task. Back to our discussion on the leadership pipeline, Self-Leaders need to be prepared for success, which involves skill training on how to do the job assigned to them, and they need ongoing support to keep them encouraged and motivated. Let me state again for emphasis: this skill training must take place *before* they are expected to do the job. No more "sink or swim" mentality. We need to train them well so we set them up for success, not failure.

Second, they need vision. They must see how their one task accomplishes a greater purpose. I heard a story about two bricklayers working on a building in downtown New York City. Someone asked the first bricklayer what he has doing. The first bricklayer responded, "I'm laying brick." Then someone asked the second bricklayer what he was doing. The second bricklayer replied, "I'm building a skyscraper!" So one bricklayer had a job, and the other had a vision.

Servers and volunteers must know their task is important. Every greeter creates a warm environment for a first-time guest to hear the gospel. Every baby rocker demonstrates God's love to the most vulnerable. Every offering counter assures the congregation that the church handles God's money with the utmost integrity. Every job matters; every role is a vital part of the whole. Paul speaks to this in 1 Corinthians 12:12–27 when he describes the church as a human body. Not all parts of the body are the same. Some body parts are clearly vital to the body's function, and some aren't as recognizably vital. Yet all are important, and the body suffers if one part is missing. This is true for every church. If servers and volunteers see how they contribute to the whole, they will serve with enthusiasm and joy.

Third, servers need spiritual encouragement. Simply assigning a task to a volunteer and missing the opportunity to invest in their lives is a big mistake. For many people, serving is an entry point to their spiritual journey. Many people who do not know Christ and even more who are young in the faith may volunteer. What better place for spiritual seekers to be than working alongside passionate Christ followers? They get to see God's family working together for a common goal and participate in it. That's amazing, isn't it? Further, serving is always a spiritual stimulator. When a person serves, they choose to be involved in God's work. This almost always leads to greater opportunities for them to take another step in their spiritual journey.

In addition, Self-Leaders need community. They need to know they are part of a team and part of a family who serves together and cares for each other. Every healthy team has great camaraderie. Each player knows each other, calls each other by name (and nicknames). They have the shared experience of serving together as they make memories together. This is what every Self-Leader needs. They need someone to know their name and if they are missing, someone to care about them and pray for them, and they need to belong.

Lastly, Self-Leaders need appreciation. You will be amazed at how a simple "Thank you" makes a person feel appreciated. A special gift. A shout-out on social media. A favorite drink or treat. All these things make a person feel acknowledged and appreciated. I've heard it said, "Volunteers are paid in appreciation dollars." This is so true.

HOW JESUS DEVELOPED SELF-LEADERS

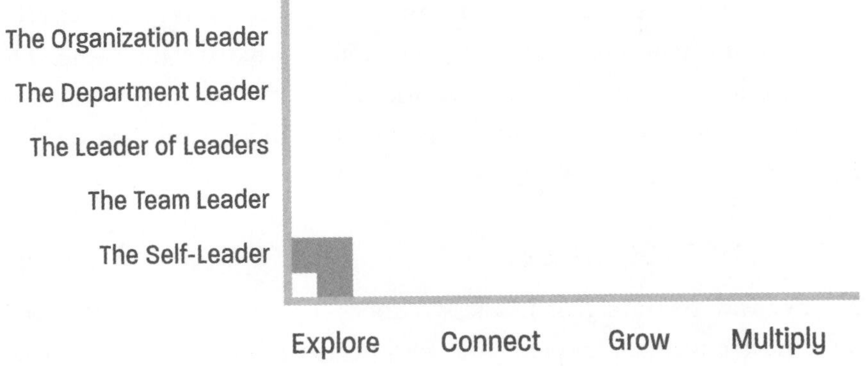

How did Jesus train up and develop Self-Leaders? We see this most clearly in the first eighteen months of Jesus' ministry. Once again, *Harmony of the Gospels* allows you to see Jesus' life and ministry from a chronological perspective. As I studied these passages, a few training elements stood out. Training Self-Leaders as Jesus did requires you to incorporate these themes into your development plan for every volunteer or server in your ministry.

CULTIVATE CURIOSITY

This is where Jesus began with his potential leaders. We saw in Chapter 3 how Jesus invited his first followers to "come and see" where he was staying (John 1:35–39). Thus, Jesus stimulated their curiosity. Later he explained even more clearly who he was and why he had come, but for now it was good for them to ask questions and seek answers for themselves.

Cultivating curiosity in new leaders is imperative. Encourage them to ask questions because seeking out answers is an integral part of their development. This starts with curiosity about their role. What is expected of them? How much time will this role require? How should they dress? To whom do they report? What should they do if things go wrong? Why is their role important to the entire vision of the church? What are the basic skills necessary to succeed in this role? So cultivate curiosity and invite questions. Also, invite new leaders to speak into the process. Ask them, "Is there a way to improve what we are doing? Do you have new ideas?" The more relational bonds you forge with new leaders, the stronger their commitment will be to your ministry and to the church.

SPEND TIME TOGETHER

Another way to train Self-Leaders is spending time with them. Jesus was a master at this. He spent time with his disciples. Immediately after calling his first five disciples, he spent time with them. He took these men to Cana to a wedding (John 2:1–11). Afterward, he took his disciples with him on a family vacation to the Sea of Galilee for a few days (John 2:12). Following that, Jesus traveled with them to Jerusalem for the Passover, where they worshiped together. Then we read, "After this, Jesus and his disciples went to the Judean countryside, where he spent time with them" (John 3:22). Clearly, Jesus spent time with his men in these early stages of development.

Now if you are a Department Leader, you might have hundreds of volunteers under your direction. You can't spend time with every volunteer outside of your ministry time together. This is why Self-Leaders are managed by Team Leaders (whom we will discuss in the next chapter). And Team Leaders are responsible to train, develop, and care for the servers on their team. As you break down large ministry departments into small ministry teams, you can begin providing the relational care and support each team member needs and deserves.

SPARK SPIRITUAL CONVERSATIONS

Some memories you can never forget. They are etched in your brain forever. Some are shocking, unexpected, even dangerous memories.

His men had been with him less than a year. They were still trying to wrap their minds around what made this rabbi so different from everyone else. As Jesus took them into the bustling city of Jerusalem for the Passover, he shocked them by flipping over the moneychangers' tables and rebuking them for turning his Father's house into a den of thieves. Then, if that wasn't enough, one of the most powerful men in the city, a member of the Sanhedrin named Nicodemus, came calling for Jesus at night. And Jesus, without hesitation, said Nicodemus must be born again (John 3:1–21). That took incredible courage, and Jesus' men never forgot it. Even though they were with Jesus, they were still formulating their understanding of who he was and why he had chosen them. These spiritual conversations were integral to their own spiritual growth and development.

As you develop Self-Leaders in your ministry, you must have spiritual conversations with them. Where are they on their own spiritual journey? What questions do they wrestle with? Can they articulate a clear time when they received Christ as Lord? Never assume a person knows Christ. In fact, if you are going to assume, assume that they don't. Why? Because every volunteer needs someone to look after their soul. They need someone to care where they stand in view of eternity. These conversations are best had one-on-one over lunch or a cup of coffee. Sometimes they can begin as simple prayer requests. I like to ask people the open question, "So what's your story?" They usually ask what I mean, and I'll say, "Start wherever you want, and end wherever you want. Just tell me your story." You will be amazed at what you will learn when you ask for someone's story. Every Team Leader should know where their team stands spiritually so they can shepherd them well.

STRETCH THEM

As you develop your volunteers, don't be afraid to stretch them beyond what they think is possible. Jesus certainly did. Within that first year, Jesus pushed his men way out of their comfort zones. Returning to Galilee after their visit to Jerusalem, Jesus directed his team to head north through Samaria. This was outside the norm for two reasons. First, the trek through Samaria was incredibly difficult. The mountains were steep and the water sparse. This is why most Jews traveled north along the Jordan River valley on level ground along a constant source of water. Also, Jews didn't travel through Samaria because of the conflict between Jews and Samaritans. Years of division and hatred made travel in that part of the country dangerous. No good Jew would ever be caught dead in Samaria. That is, except for Jesus, who had business there (John 4:4).

While in Samaria, Jesus spoke to an outcast woman drawing water in the heat of the day. This again was way outside the bounds for most Jewish men in that day. Men didn't speak to women, certainly not a Samaritan woman (John 4:27). And then there was her reputation. Men didn't speak to *those* kinds of women, but Jesus broke down barriers. He broke down cultural and racial barriers and deep-seeded prejudices and animosities that had caused some people to be seen as deplorable or less than human. And when the disciples asked if Jesus wanted something to eat, Jesus said reaching people and doing his Father's work were his food, his nourishment, and his satisfaction (John 4:34–38). These were teachable moments, where Jesus stretched his men to think differently, act differently, and see the world through a whole new lens.

LOOK FOR WAYS TO STRETCH YOUR VOLUNTEERS.

Look for ways to stretch your volunteers. Stretch their thinking by asking questions that cause them to think deeper. Stretch them spiritually by asking them to lead team devotions or prayer meetings. Stretch their leadership by asking if they would consider stepping up to another level of leadership. Stretch their vision by asking them to dream bigger. And while you are stretching them, stress that you believe in them and that God has bigger plans for them than they even realize.

DEFUSE NEGATIVITY

Invariably, people who serve will encounter someone negative. That person who doesn't want to follow an usher's direction. That parent who is upset about their child's care. That member who thinks the music is too loud or the lights are too dim. Someone is always unhappy about something. How will your Self-Leaders handle negative people?

Jesus taught his men how to defuse these situations. Toward the end of this stage of development, Jesus took his men to his hometown of Nazareth. Everyone was excited to see this local man who had suddenly become a celebrity. They invited Jesus to read from the scroll in the synagogue, and everyone's eyes fixated on him. Jesus read the Isaiah 61 passage that describes the ministry of the promised Messiah. Then he said, "Today as you listen, this Scripture has been fulfilled" (Luke 4:21). His words first surfaced questions but then quickly gave way to anger and outright rejection. They laid their hands on Jesus and dragged him out of the town to push him over a cliff. His disciples must have been shocked at how these religious people had turned negative so quickly, yet Jesus evaded their grasp as he "passed right through the crowd and went on his way" (Luke 4:30). This was not the last time his disciples would encounter negative people.

The same is true with your volunteers. Because volunteers are usually the people in direct contact with guests and church members, they are the ones most likely to encounter negative people. As you train your volunteers, coach them on how to handle negative people. Draft up scenarios, role play, and brainstorm ways to defuse situations. Also train them on how to recognize when situations are escalating and whom to contact for help. Doing this will empower your volunteers to serve courageously and help each other along the way.

UNDER THE RADAR

Training up Self-Leaders is vital to both your ministry and the overall ministry of the church. Don't take them for granted. In fact, look for those key leaders hiding in volunteer positions. When Jesus drafted his first leaders, he knew what they were capable of doing. He could see potential, he could perceive their leadership gifts, and he drew those gifts to the surface. As you shepherd the volunteers under your care, look for the potential hidden in each of them. Many people may serve in your area of ministry who are capable of leading at a much higher level. They lead at key levels in their businesses and schools, but they remain under the radar in the church. Make it your aim to find the greater potential and draw it to the surface.

Here's an example. Brenda started attending church after her divorce. The pain and disappointment caused her to examine her life and the direction of it. One Sunday morning, after hearing the gospel preached, she asked Jesus to forgive her sins and lead her life. Soon she joined a group of believers who met every Sunday to study the Bible and encourage each other. Her heart hungered for community, and she saw families facing the same struggles she faced; however, something was missing. She felt awkward being in a group of mostly married couples while she was single again. But an older woman in the group took Brenda under her wing and discipled her personally.

The next several months were transformational for Brenda. She started growing in her walk with Christ, learning to read the Bible on her own, and maturing in her prayer life. She started seeing people through an eternal lens and taking bold steps to share what God was doing in her life. Along the way she volunteered in her group and served in various community projects. God was truly at work in her life.

Six months later, God started stirring Brenda's heart to start a group for single mothers like herself. She wanted others to find the peace and community she had found through her church. Despite feeling inadequate to lead a group, she was encouraged by a pastor at the church and others in her group to step out in faith and trust God to work through her. When she launched her group, she was amazed at the response. Ten single moms walked through the door, many of whom had felt alone and ostracized, each one with a story to tell and a desperate need for God's love. Brenda discovered that God could use even the pains of her past as a platform to point people to Jesus and show God's love.

Finding people like Brenda in your church isn't difficult; it just takes intentionality. And developing Self-Leaders like Brenda is vital to any church or ministry. After all, you have more of these people than anyone else. Your church is filled with volunteers who come faithfully and serve joyfully. How many of them could rise up to be significant leadership in your church if they were developed and inspired? Most of your "leadership gold" can be mined from this rock.

Jesus developed leaders at this level by stimulating their curiosity for more and inviting them to "come and see" what he was all about. He worked hard to create a sense of belonging and community on his team, and he sparked spiritual conversations. Last, he taught how to defuse negative people. Along the way he constantly looked for who was getting it, who was growing, and who could move to the next level of leadership. As you develop the Self-Leaders on your team, you will no doubt have some great spiritual conversations. Who knows? You may be privileged to lead some to faith in Jesus. You will also find many eager to lead at the next level.

So what is the next level of leadership? That's what the next chapter is all about.

GROUP DISCUSSION QUESTIONS

1. When you think of Self-Leaders, what comes to mind?
2. What do volunteers need from their Team Leaders?
3. What is your best strategy for finding and engaging new volunteers?
4. Which of the elements of Jesus' training stand out most to you? Why?
5. How can you spark spiritual conversations with volunteers?

DISCIPLE-MAKING MOVEMENT PROFILE

The Suffering Movement

Dietrich Bonhoeffer was born in 1906 to a wealthy, extraordinary family. His father, Karl, was the most recognized psychiatrist in Germany in the early part of the twentieth century. His mother, Paula, was an intellectual in her own right as a prominent educator in a day when women seldom held such standing in the community. His brothers and sisters were intellectually curious and successful in their various fields. Bonhoeffer also shared the family acumen for academics, choosing to study theology as a young teenager.

At the age of seventeen he entered the historic Tübingen University to begin his studies, and he later transferred to Berlin University, where he earned a doctorate at the age of twenty-one. Shortly thereafter, a trip to New York City radically shaped Bonhoeffer's heart and mind. A fellow student invited him to attend the Abyssinian Baptist Church in Harlem, where he saw people worshiping God with passion and deep devotion. The sermons were fiery, pressing people to love Jesus more than anything else.

This was a very different experience than what he had growing up in the Lutheran churches of Germany.

Returning to Berlin to teach at the university, he was clearly different. He began referring to the Bible as "God's Word." He often took his students away on retreats and taught them to pray. Dietrich even asked one student, "Do you love Jesus?"[30] Bonhoeffer realized that a true devotion to Jesus impacts every part of a person's life. Such devotion leads to life change and to action congruent with that belief, regardless of the consequences.

As his passion for Christ grew, he could see the coming political storm brewing on the horizon. In January 1933, Bonhoeffer gave his first public speech opposing Hitler's leadership philosophy. He realized that Hitler despised the church and sought to infiltrate it from within, turning its focus from the gospel and its Jewish roots to nationalism. In response, Bonhoeffer led a group of pastors to establish the Confessing Church to hold fast to biblical truth. During this time, he wrote such classics as *Life Together* and *The Cost of Discipleship*, portraying the Christian life as one of deep community and steadfast commitment to Christ regardless of the cost.

Bonhoeffer became convinced that only the removal of Hitler would stop the advance of evil. He and several family members collaborated within the elitist circles of Berlin to remove or kill the Fuhrer. Eventually, he was arrested for assisting a small group of Jews in escaping Germany. He was initially placed in the Tegel military prison, just seven miles from his home. During this time, he wrote *Letters and Papers from Prison* and his famous poem "Who Am I?"

Bonhoeffer was not afraid to die. For him, true devotion to Christ required sacrifice. *The Cost of Discipleship* states, "When Christ calls a man, he bids him come and die."[31]

Bonhoeffer was hanged to death on April 9, 1945, in Flossenbürg concentration camp, just three weeks before the end of the war. His legacy is a call to discipleship that is real and unrelenting in the face of evil, requiring a willingness to give it all to follow Jesus.

7

DEVELOPING TEAM LEADERS

People don't leave a company; they leave their boss. If you have ever left a job, you know that's true. A bad boss can make life miserable, and I can relate. One summer while I was in college, I worked for the highway department in central Texas. I started out as a flagman, directing traffic to slow down around the construction sites scattered down the long ribbon of highway that stretched between College Station and Houston. It was a mindless job, to be honest, and it was hot. Our crew was also responsible for shoveling hot mix (a 350-degree mixture of molten asphalt and gravel) and pouring liquid tar to fill cracks and potholes on the roads. Did I say it was hot?

The work was dirty and gritty, but my team leader made it awful. This man was small in stature, probably no more than five feet, six inches in height, with a thin, skeleton-like frame. The sun had leathered his skin. He had no teeth and no dentures, so when he closed his mouth, his chin nearly touched the tip of his nose. And his language would make a navy sailor blush with embarrassment. He loved to say, "I'm here to teach you college boys (dragging those words out loud and long "coooolllege boyz") how to work." His personal mission was making sure we got the proper education in sweat and tears. He was a terrible team leader. He didn't know us by name. He yelled and cussed a lot but didn't train us for the job. All he cared about was how miserable he could make us.

This guy was the polar opposite of a manager I had in high school. During my senior year, I worked at a men's clothier. I was happy to have the job since up to that point most of my work had consisted of mowing lawns or working out in the fields. Two brothers owned the business and were hands-on in operating the store. Max, the older of the two, was funny. He loved practical jokes and teasing his team. Every Saturday morning when I showed up for work after a Friday night football game, Max had his take on the game. He also trained me on how to pair up coats and ties, slacks and shirts, the difference between certain fabrics, and the proper way to help a man try on shoes. He helped me master the skill of working the cash register and closing out at the end of the day. He often took an interest in my life and offered godly counsel. Still to this day, I look back on those days at the men's store with appreciation for his investment in my life.

The two team leaders I just described could not be further apart. One knew me personally and cared about my life. The other didn't even know my name. One encouraged me to learn new things and grow, and the other talked down to me and took pleasure in my failures. One was a great team leader, and the other was a horrible team leader. The same is true in a church. There are some great team leaders, and others who are not so great. But as goes the team leader, so goes the team.

LEADING THE TEAM

Team Leaders set the pace for every organization or ministry. They can make the environment toxic or positive. They can raise up the next generation of leaders or force them out the door to work for someone else. This is why so much success in ministry rises or falls on Team Leaders doing their job well. In the last chapter, we looked at the role of Self-Leaders, those who do the tasks that need to be done. We saw what these leaders need and how to develop them. And that work of development is the work of the Team Leader.

> **TEAM LEADERS SET THE PACE FOR EVERY ORGANIZATION OR MINISTRY.**

Here is a simple definition of a Team Leader from a ministry context: a Team Leader is a volunteer who leads a team of people to accomplish multiple ministry tasks. Your church or ministry is filled with Team Leaders. They lead a small group, a prayer team, or a team to set up or tear down after an event. They run the worship rehearsal or direct the Communion team. They are the greeter captains, the band leaders, technology leaders, home team leaders, the missions team leaders, or even the head deacons. Your church is full of Team Leaders. They are usually volunteers, meaning they are not paid staff, and their primary role is to lead the team to be successful in doing the work at hand.

The size of these teams may vary depending on the specific ministry tasks, but they could be anywhere from two to fifty people. But the important, big shift is from doing the work themselves to accomplishing the work through a team. Team Leaders focus on the teams they lead, not just what needs to be done. Prior to this, they were Self-Leaders. They were proficient at accomplishing tasks. Now Team Leaders lead others to do the work. This is a very different skill, and not everyone can make that transition.

One young man in our ministry was particularly gifted at community engagement and sharing his faith. He was likeable and skilled at moving conversations toward the gospel. He became so proficient at it that we asked him to lead a team doing what he did. However, over time it became clear that while this young man was a great volunteer, he was not a great leader. He was often unclear of what his team needed to know because what came instinctively to him was not instinctive to others. He struggled to train and organize. Instead of coaching others and identifying emerging leaders, he did everything himself. Thus, this shift from doing to leading is a big one. Not everyone can make it. The Team

Leader must derive their joy and satisfaction from the team accomplishing the work, not the leader doing it.

THE GOOD, THE BAD, AND THE UGLY

Most likely you have had some great team leaders and some really poor ones too. What separates them? What do good Team Leaders do? What do bad Team Leaders do? And what is the worst thing you can do if you lead a team? We will reserve that one for the close of this chapter.

Good Team Leaders

- Organize the work for the team.
- Invite input from their team.
- Delegate clearly and appropriately.
- Inspire their team.
- Take responsibility for problems and fix them.
- Communicate well.
- Care about their team members.
- Observe and offer feedback.
- Set the team up for success.
- Are patient.
- Cast a vision of why the team's work is important.
- Appreciate the team.
- Confront issues head on.
- Encourage the team spiritually.
- Make the work fun.
- Elevate team members to higher leadership roles.

Bad Team Leaders

- Are disorganized and frantic.
- Think their way is the only way.
- Do the job themselves.
- Create a hostile environment.
- Make excuses and blame others.
- Don't communicate well.
- Aren't interested in anything but the job.
- Criticize and don't offer solutions.
- Set the team up to fail.
- Are combative.
- Think small.
- Are never satisfied.
- Avoid conflict.
- Ignore spiritual issues.
- Make the work unbearable.
- Hold people down.

Seeing juxtaposed qualities on a chart brings clarity and contrast. When I think about Max and my highway department manager, the differences could not be clearer. Max was clearly a good leader, the other one was bad.

This list also provides a great starting point for those training Team Leaders. It is the responsibility of the Leaders of Leaders to train Team Leaders. As we will discuss in the next chapter, Leaders of Leaders are tasked with recruiting, assessing, preparing, and supporting Team Leaders. What this requires, first and foremost, is a written job description of what you expect from your Team Leaders. When things are written down, they are important. Training also requires some basic equipping in delegation, communication, confronting problems, and spiritual investment. Along the way, set regular times to observe your Team Leaders with their teams and offer constructive feedback and coaching.

HOW DID JESUS DEVELOP TEAM LEADERS?

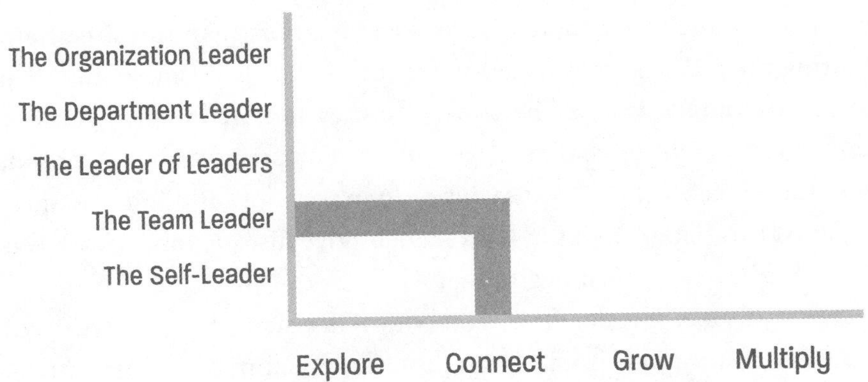

How did Jesus raise up Team Leaders who shared his heart and vision? Digging into the second part of Jesus' disciple-making pathway, we find crucial lessons for developing Team Leaders. Jesus called his men to a higher level of leadership (what I consider to be the second level of leadership); however, he didn't release them to lead teams immediately. He would release them to multiply and lead teams in the future, but first they needed his heart before they could be successful. So Jesus invested six months of his life involving these men in his ministry and shaping their view of the world and Christlike leadership. If you want to raise up great Team Leaders, follow Jesus' example.

CAST VISION

It is vital to cast vision as you develop Team Leaders. They need to have a proper vision of where the church is headed, their role in this process, and how the teams they lead fit into the overall vision of the church. Why is this so critical? Because you are training these Team Leaders to be leaders, not doers. Their primary role is to lead the team to accomplish the tasks, not do the work themselves. Understanding this big shift requires big vision.

In the middle of Matthew 4, Jesus was in a transition of his own. For the past eighteen months, Jesus had recruited his initial followers and invited both skeptics and believers to "come and see" what he was about. His band of men were more like weekend warriors than full-time staff. During the evenings they fished as part of the family business, and then in the afternoons and on the weekends, they followed their rabbi. But things were about to change. After John the Baptist was put in prison, the time came for Jesus to step out of John's shadow and into the spotlight. At this critical point in God's redemptive history, John's work was done, but Jesus' was just beginning.

At this time, Jesus made several critical decisions. First, he relocated his base of operations from Nazareth to Capernaum, a lively city strategically located on the northern edge of the Sea of Galilee and along an international trade route. Second, Jesus began to preach publicly, filling the role John the Baptist had vacated as the leader of the budding movement. And third, Jesus began calling his leaders to a whole new level of commitment.

Walking along the shore in the morning, after the night of fishing was done and the men were maintaining their nets, Jesus spoke to Peter and Andrew. "Follow me, . . . and I will make you fish for people"

(Matt. 4:19). Immediately these men left their nets and followed Jesus. Later seeing James and John, the sons of Zebedee, doing the same, Jesus called them as well, and they too left their nets to follow Jesus. Leaving their nets was so incredibly important that its significance cannot be overstated. It was a conscious decision to leave their families, their identities, and their source of income to follow Jesus. It'd be like walking off the job and selling your home to follow a preacher.

This was a big decision. How did they make this decision so quickly? Remember, they had been following Jesus off and on for a year and a half. I'm sure they knew this day would come. Also keep in mind that most of these disciples, except for Peter, were teenagers who had few obligations and could travel light. For one of them to be chosen to follow a rabbi like Jesus would have brought great honor to their families.

But what intrigues me the most is not *that* Jesus called his men to a higher commitment, but *how* he did it. All night these men had cast their nets in the sea, hoping to draw in tilapia on the moonlit surface of the water. Now Jesus was casting a net of his own by casting a greater vision. And this greater vision drew these men to himself like steel to a magnet. Read Jesus' words again: "Follow me, . . . and I will make you fish for people." In other words, "Men, your fathers were fishermen, as were their fathers before them, and their fathers before them. Your whole life is wrapped around catching these fish. But if you follow me, I will give you a greater purpose for your life. Instead of catching fish, you will catch people!" Jesus tapped into the hidden desire in every person to live a life of significance. That desire is in both you and me. We want our lives to have meaning.

Those you train as Team Leaders have jobs and families. They have deadlines and meetings as well. They have families with needs and the daily pressures of life. But deep inside they want to know their lives matter. They want to leave behind something significant. A man once said if you stick your hand in a bucket of water, and then pull it out, the hole left behind is the measure of your impact in this world. Sounds cynical, doesn't it? But for some, their greatest fear is that they're insignificant.

Basically, Jesus came along and said, "Follow me and you will make an eternal difference!" No wonder the disciples left everything to follow him. So start with casting a vision. Make sure your Team Leaders know what they do makes an eternal difference. Make sure they realize their lives matter, their ministry matters, and their influence on their team matters. Cast a big vision of a big God who promises to do big things through them if they will join Jesus in his big plan to reach the world.

MAKE SURE YOUR TEAM LEADERS KNOW WHAT THEY DO MAKES AN ETERNAL DIFFERENCE.

GET THEM OUT OF THE BUILDING

After Jesus called his disciples to this new level of commitment, they began engaging in Jesus' ministry. Dann Spader likes to say that Jesus took the disciples on six "fishing trips," which are recorded in Luke's Gospel. They first fished for people at the synagogue where Jesus a demon out of a possessed man (Luke 4:31–37). Next, they fished among the sick and hurting. Jesus healed Peter's mother-in-law, and many others showed up to be healed and delivered from demonic oppression (Luke 4:38–41), after which Jesus took his men on a mission trip of sorts, touring neighboring villages and preaching the gospel (Luke 4:42–44). The third fishing trip is in Luke 5:1–11 where Jesus miraculously filled their boats with fish for all to see. Fishing trip number four was the healing of a leper (Luke 5:12–16). Number five was the healing of a paralytic (Luke 5:17–26), and the final trip was the call of Matthew (Luke 5:27–32). In each of these cases, Jesus did the heavy lifting. He did the miracles. He was the center of attention and focus, but the disciples still played a part.

When Jesus called his men to a higher level of leadership commitment, he didn't stick them in a classroom. He didn't say, "So, guys, we are going to meet for the next twelve months at the synagogue, and I'm going to take you through a few scrolls." Instead, he got them out of the building and showed them where God was at work. He wanted them to experience firsthand God's working in a powerful way. Your Team

Leaders don't need another seminar; they need to see God at work. They don't need another Bible study; they need to be exposed to the power of God in such a palpable way that they are transformed. This isn't some kind of charismatic experience: it's seeing how God changes lives.

Remember Zach in Chapter 4? Part of his story is how going on mission trips to Zambia dramatically impacted him and how he could see that his life made an eternal difference. That is what your Team Leaders need to see. They need to see it, smell it, taste it, and hear it. Why? Because seeing God at work will give them a hunger for God to use them in a powerful way for the rest of their lives.

How did Jesus do this? He led them into their community. Invite your Team Leaders to join you in ministry in your own community. Take them to a local homeless shelter to share your faith. Take them to hand out backpacks to needy kids in the fall. Take them to pray for teachers and principals in your neighborhoods. Take them to have lunch with a businessman. Take them on a short-term mission trip. The key is to *take them*! Join God in what he is doing, and then talk about what that would look like in their life.

Jesus effectively told his men, "Okay, men, let's go!" and they followed him. You need to do the same. Take your Team Leaders where they can see God at work, and it will change their lives forever. The disciples were never the same, and your Team Leaders won't be either.

GO DEEP TO GO WIDE

In all the hustle and bustle of ministry, Jesus still found time to be with his Father. It's easy for the pace of life to squeeze out what's most important. Have you ever said to yourself, *I've got so much work today. I don't have time to read God's Word and pray. I'll pick it up tomorrow.* We've all done that from time to time, but not Jesus. The busier life got, the more determined Jesus was to go deeper in prayer with his Father.

We see this in Mark's Gospel as Jesus had just been up until late in the night healing the sick, casting out demons, caring for hurting people. I'm sure at the end of the day he was completely exhausted. If there was a day to hit the snooze button, it would have been that day. But no, Jesus was up early:

> Very early in the morning, while it was still dark, he got up, went out, and made his way to a deserted place; and there he was praying. Simon and his companions searched for him, and when they found him they said, "Everyone is looking for you." And he said to them, "Let's go on to the neighboring villages so that I may preach there too. This is why I have come." He went into all of Galilee, preaching in their synagogues and driving out demons. (Mark 1:35–39)

Why is this important? Jesus modeled for his men an important principle: you must go deep to go wide. The deeper you go in prayer, in God's Word, and in knowing and following Jesus, the deeper God will use you to advance his kingdom. A lot of people get this one backward. They think if they focus on how wide their ministry will go, then it will result in a deeper walk with God. But that is not the case. The deep things of God produce the wide reach of ministry.

Chuck Swindoll underscores this desperate need for a deeper walk with God. He recalled a pastor who came up to him following a meeting and confessed, "I'm operating on fumes. I am lonely, hollow, shallow, enslaved to a schedule that never lets up." Reflecting on that man's honest and vulnerable confession, Swindoll writes:

> As a result of my observations and that recent encounter specifically, I decided to do some serious thinking and reading and praying. My journal became the anvil on which most of my private thoughts were hammered out. Thankfully, I have had the time to let those thoughts linger and spawn other thoughts that drove me deeper until I arrived at the heart of what seems to be the core issue—a lack of intimacy. Pure and simple, that best defines the problem. An absence of intimacy with the Almighty.

> Involvements, yes, but no intimacy. Activities and programs aplenty, but not intimacy.[32]

Swindoll's observations are on point with the struggles of most ministry leaders. The pace, the perfection, and the performance expected of ministries leaders often create the perfect storm that causes many to put on the appearance of spiritual health while inwardly they struggle.

Your Team Leaders must learn this now. Neglecting their personal walk with God will hinder their ministry and put their soul in danger.

Many pastors who chase after the lure of a sweeping, wide ministry to the neglect of their intimacy with Christ will find the ground give way as the erosion of their souls causes them to fall into personal sin.

Jesus didn't give in to the swell of popularity. He didn't chase after society's approval. Being a celebrity didn't entice him. He walked with his Father and was focused on the Father's will.

Toward the end of his ministry, Jesus surfaced the need for intimacy with the Father again. Under the glowing light of the moon, Jesus led his men toward the Garden of Gethsemane, and he stopped to examine a grapevine. He said, "I am the vine; you are the branches. The one who remains in me and I in him produces much fruit, because you can do nothing without me" (John 15:5). Just as Jesus was dependent on his Father, Jesus' followers must be dependent on him. This deeper life is found in ongoing intimacy with Jesus. Your Team Leaders need to grow in this area. And this is a tremendous opportunity to disciple these Team Leaders and show them how to feed themselves with God's Word, how to put Jesus at the center of their lives, and how to pray effectively and passionately. Teach them how to pursue holiness and run from compromise. Show them how to walk in grace and pursue biblical community. You must go deep to go wide.

HELP THEM TAKE STEPS OF FAITH

As you walk with God, sometimes you hit a roadblock. It may be doubt . . . pain . . . a hurried life . . . an internal struggle. Whatever it is, this roadblock stands in the way of your full surrender to Jesus. And as long as this roadblock exists, you are at a standstill. In reality, relationships are never neutral. You are either advancing or retreating. Moving forward or falling behind.

This was the case with Peter. In those early months, he was taken aback by Jesus. He knew this rabbi was not like the others: his words were the words of life. Peter had seen him perform miracles. He experienced a rush of excitement and thrill he had never felt before. And after Jesus called him to be his follower, Peter left his nets to follow his rabbi. Peter was all in. But then reality settled in. Peter had a job, a wife, and a mother-in-law. How would he take care of those who depended on him if he left to follow Jesus? These may have been nagging thoughts in the back of his mind, or they could have been honest conversations in his home at night.

The two responsibilities of caring for his family and following Jesus were different roads heading in opposite directions. After a night of fishing with nothing to show for it except a knot in his stomach and worries on his mind, Peter was asked by Jesus to throw his net out for a catch. Peter reminded Jesus that he had worked hard all night and caught nothing. "We've worked hard all night long and caught nothing. But if you say so, I'll let down the nets" (Luke 5:5). Notice that last part? "If you say so, I will." That was Peter's heart. That's what Jesus loved about him, a trustful surrender to follow.

Peter threw his net out in broad daylight, with everyone watching, and waited. Then suddenly the waters began churning and frothing, the tiny fishing boat began listing downward, groaning under the weight. Soon so many fish filled his net that he needed help to drag it all in. It was a miracle and the greatest catch of his life! This meant more money than he could imagine. And the thrill of the moment was immediately interrupted by the sharp pain of guilt. He knew his heart was considering turning back because of his pressure to provide. And looking at Jesus, Peter knew that Jesus knew it too. Peter fell at Jesus' feet, confessing, "Go away from me, because I'm a sinful man, Lord!" (Luke 5:8). But Jesus assured him, "Don't be afraid. . . . From now on you will be catching people" (Luke 5:10). After this, the disciples went ashore, left everything behind, and followed Jesus.

Jesus knows what holds you back. He knows what races through your mind or keeps you up at night. He's not taken aback by your struggles or disappointed in your doubts. Quite the opposite. He wants to move in those doubts and struggles in ways that will cause you to trust him even more. At this point, Peter never looked back. He knew he could trust Jesus to provide all he needed, not only for him but for his family as well. As you talk with your Team Leaders about going deeper with Jesus, help them identify the areas of their lives where they don't trust Jesus fully. We all carry doubts and distractions that can keep us from living our fullest life for him. These early victories of faith will provide the confidence to trust Jesus for bigger battles ahead.

CULTIVATE A SHEPHERD'S HEART

The balance of this development phase in Jesus' strategy wraps around three separate episodes of conflict. Not conflict on his team but conflict with the religious leaders. Already Jesus drew both supporters and critics. Some were drawn to him, and others were repulsed by him. One of the consistent areas of conflict revolved around the Sabbath laws. According to Sabbath regulations, no work could be done, yet Jesus constantly challenged the rigidity of those laws, especially when healing on the Sabbath brought hope and healing to the broken. In John 5:10–18 Jesus healed a man who had been crippled from birth. But this amazing miracle received a sharp rebuke by the Pharisees, who chastised the man for carrying his mat on the Sabbath. Jesus confronted their hard hearts: "The works which the Father has given Me to accomplish—the very works that I do—testify about Me, that the Father has sent Me" (John 5:36, NASB). These Pharisees couldn't see past their rules to see the miracle worker who stared them in the face.

On another occasion, Jesus and his disciples traveled through a wheatfield on the Sabbath. Because they were hungry, they picked a few grains from the heads of wheat for a quick snack. Again, the Pharisees cried foul saying, "Why are you doing what is unlawful on the Sabbath?" (Luke 6:2, NIV). Picking grain wasn't unlawful but working on the Sabbath was unlawful. And the picking of a few pieces of grain was considered harvesting. Jesus reminded them that he was the "Lord of the Sabbath" (Luke 6:2, NIV).

But another episode happened that was worse than any so far. The Pharisees, looking to get rid of Jesus, invited him to speak in the synagogue on the Sabbath. And there, on the front row, was a man with a withered hand. They knew Jesus was a sucker for hurting people. If he healed this man on the Sabbath, the Pharisees could bring charges against him. But Jesus knew what was happening. He asked the man to stand up in front of everyone. Then Jesus posed a question directly to the crowd. "Is it lawful on the Sabbath to do good or to do harm, to save a life or to kill?" (Mark 3:4, ESV). The room was silent. Then we read, "After looking around at them with anger, he was grieved at the hardness of their hearts and told the man, 'Stretch out your hand'" (Mark 3:5). What grieved Jesus was the Pharisees' hard hearts. They had become so focused on rules that they lost a heart for people.

This is a danger for any leader. It's easy as a Team Leader to fixate on rules, expectations, and team performance, and forget the more important things such as kindness, compassion, and mercy. Jesus never wanted his men to become desensitized to the hurts of people. He wanted them to have his shepherd's heart, which he later reinforced: "I am the good shepherd. The good shepherd lays down his life for the sheep" (John 10:11). When he healed the man with a withered hand, Jesus knew that act of compassion would eventually cost him his life.

But that's what shepherds do: they lay down their lives for the sheep. The same is true today. We need more shepherds like Jesus. Less rule following, more compassion. Less offense, more grace. This isn't an appeal to be lax on sin; Jesus certainly wasn't. Yet we should reflect Jesus' heart that loves the hurting, cares for the broken, and sacrifices for the outcast. That's a shepherd's heart.

MIRRORS

As you develop Team Leaders, there is certainly a need for skill training. As I mentioned earlier in this chapter, there is work to be done in delegation, communication, organization, coaching, feedback, and the like. All of these are necessary to be a great Team Leader. But in this phase of ministry, Jesus worked more on the inside than he did the outside. He developed men who were like him at heart. All the skill development cannot replace the need in a leader's life for godly vision, compassion for people, great faith, and a deep walk with God. These are the foundations upon which higher levels of leadership are built. So we must work on the foundations. We must cultivate the heart of the leader. We must constantly hold up Jesus as our example and hold ourselves up to his standard to see where we fall short.

Earlier I mentioned the good, the bad, and the ugly parts of being a Team Leader. I laid out the good and the bad, but here is the ugly. The ugliest Team Leader is one who doesn't reflect the heart of Jesus, one who has forgotten they serve and represent Jesus. Yet Jesus looks for leaders who are mirrors that reflect his shepherd's heart and his love to the people around them.

Developing Team Leaders is essential to the growth and health of your ministry. They set the tone for the ministry and reflect its culture. This is why so much rides on the Team Leaders of any church or ministry organization. As go your Team Leaders, so goes the ministry. And this is why Jesus spent so much time, during the first stage of his ministry training, developing his men to mirror his heart of ministry. He helped them see the greater vision God had for their lives. He moved them out of the building and fostered environments where they engaged in hands-on ministry. Jesus was never about seeking position but always about touching and caring for people. He challenged his men to go deep and take high-risk steps of faith and obedience. Last, Jesus imprinted on his men a shepherd's heart to love those they lead with compassion and grace. Only with this kind of solid foundation could his men grow into leaders of a global movement.

These are the kinds of leaders needed today. Can you imagine if every one of the Team Leaders in your church modeled these characteristics of Jesus? The impact they would have on every life they touched? Jesus could. He knew with this kind of leadership foundation he could raise up men and women who would not only lead well but could also lead other leaders to do the same. And that is what we are going to discover in the next chapter.

GROUP DISCUSSION QUESTIONS

1. What is the primary role of the Team Leader?
2. Describe a time when you worked alongside a good Team Leader. What made them impactful?
3. What are some of the ways Jesus developed Team Leaders?
4. Why did Jesus get his team leadership out of the building to experience God at work? How can you do this with your Team Leaders?
5. How can you invest spiritually in your Team Leaders? What would that look like?

DISCIPLE-MAKING MOVEMENT PROFILE

The Campus Movement

Campus Crusade for Christ, founded by Bill Bright, has a worldwide reach, with 26,000 staff members leading 225,000 volunteers in over 191 different countries. Few parachurch organizations have such an expansive global presence.

But this international ministry grew from humble beginnings. The founder, Bill Bright, was born on October 19, 1921, in Coweta, Oklahoma, a small town nestled among the trees and creeks of northeast Oklahoma. Bill met his wife, Vonette, while in high school, and he later graduated from Northeastern State University. Bill had big dreams, and those dreams eventually led him away from Oklahoma to the fast-paced world of Hollywood. There Bill established a small business and began attending the First Presbyterian Church of Hollywood, where his passion for Jesus grew through the church's growing ministry to young adults.

Soon Bill sensed an ever-present burden and call to ministry. He enrolled in Princeton Theological Seminary in New Jersey, and when the commute was too much, he transferred to Fuller Seminary in California. One evening Bill and Vonette sat down and wrote what would later be called their "contract with God," surrendering all they had and all their dreams to the lordship of Jesus Christ. Bill declared himself a bondslave to Jesus and promised that he would do whatever his Master asked.[33]

Soon thereafter, God put on Bill's heart the vision for Campus Crusade for Christ. The ministry launched on the UCLA campus. It was founded on two priorities: the enthusiastic sharing of the gospel with students and the effective discipling of new believers so they could share their faith and disciple others. In its beginning stages, the ministry surveyed college students to ascertain their spiritual conditions. As Bill read the surveys, he kept repeating under his breath, "They just don't know. They just don't know." He put the surveys down and began to weep. His heart broke for these students who did not know the Lord and were so far from God. In time, the ministry quickly grew.

In 1956 Bill authored *The Four Spiritual Laws*, an evangelistic booklet. Today this booklet has been translated into more than 200 languages and 2.5 billion copies have been distributed around the world. In 1972 Bill organized EXPLO '72, a massive gathering of 85,000 students in Dallas, Texas, to hear the gospel and commit to making disciples. EXPLO '74 in South Korea drew crowds of more than 1.5 million people. In 1978 Bill partnered with film experts to produce *The Jesus Film*, a full-length film of the life of Jesus, which has been viewed by 5.1 billion people in 1400 languages and 225 countries around the world.

The expansive ministry of Campus Crusade for Christ continues to this day to live out the passion of Bill and Vonette—to make disciples of all nations until Christ returns.[34]

8

DEVELOPING LEADERS OF LEADERS

General Stanley McChrystal was at the head of the table when some of the most important decisions were made in the war against terror. From September 2003 to February 2006, he commanded the Joint Special Operations Command, which was tasked with finding and capturing high-value targets in Afghanistan and Iraq. Former defense secretary Robert Gates called McChrystal "the finest warrior and leader of men in combat I ever met."[35] However, McChrystal quickly discovered that changes needed to be made. The vastly superior US military struggled against the loosely networked, independent terror cells that always seemed to be one step ahead of the robust war machine. This led him to transform his forces into what he later called a "team of teams," combining centralized communication with a decentralized leadership authority. This innovative approach required team leaders to operate and communicate at higher levels than ever before. On a much smaller scale, this is what Leaders of Leaders are asked to do—organize and give direction to a team of teams.

Training for Leaders of Leaders is unfortunately sparse in most organizations. This is especially true within a ministry context. Most ministries begin with a pastor or church planter who does everything. He works predominantly through a small team of volunteers to pull off the most vital tasks every week. Eventually, the church grows enough for him to hire an associate, who basically does all the other jobs the pastor doesn't want to do or can't get around to doing. This pattern of staff growth continues as the church begins to add specialists, such as a kids pastor or students pastor or worship pastor. In most cases, these people lead the teams themselves. However, for the church to grow, this layer of leadership must be developed so Department Leaders can give attention to entire departments, a topic we will discuss in the next chapter.

So who are these Leaders of Leaders? What is their primary purpose? How do you find them? How do you lead them? And why are they often an overlooked yet vital element to your ministry's growth?

THE SECRET LINK

Leaders of Leaders are either high-impact volunteer coordinators or paid ministry associates whose primary purpose is to give leadership to multiple Team Leaders and help them solve problems and accomplish their ministry goals. While their actual direct reports (i.e., the Team Leaders they serve) may be only two to ten people, their leadership influence could impact over one hundred people. In most church organizational structures, this person sits in the middle. Below them are the Team Leaders and the Self-Leaders. Above them are the Department Leaders and Organization Leaders. This may not seem to be a great place to be; however, this position is strategically positioned as the ministry's secret link to success. Let me explain.

First, Leaders of Leaders are crucial to communication that runs both up and down the leadership pipeline. Problems that Team Leaders face may never find the ear of senior leadership without the Leader of Leaders communicating their needs clearly and swiftly. Likewise, new initiatives and fresh vision may not be understood or embraced by Team

Leaders and Self-Leaders without the Leader of Leaders implementing these priorities into every team. This position is the great communicator. Without this position, a huge disconnect can develop between those who set direction and those who make things happen.

Second, the Leader of Leaders ensures that things get done. Since they are in direct contact with Department Leaders, these Leaders of Leaders know what initiatives take priority and what things must happen when. They then can make sure these priorities are passed down to every team.

Third, the Leader of Leaders serves as quality control. While Department and Organization Leaders may not notice a slip in quality from the teams, the Leader of Leaders is up to speed on the current condition of the team under them and has set measures in place to solve problems and improve performance. So this position is critical to missional success.

A CERTAIN SET OF SKILLS

In a ministry context, Leaders of Leaders are found in every department. They are small group coaches who lead five to ten small group leaders. They are production assistants who coordinate the efforts of multiple teams, such as sound, lights, and video. They are women's ministry leaders who oversee multiple teams, such as special events, Bible studies, and disciple-making groups. These Leaders of Leaders must be developed, encouraged, and empowered to make decisions as they lead their team of teams. So what skills do these leaders need? Of course, they must first be proven Team Leaders and have all the skills that apply to that role. If someone has not led a team successfully, how can they lead a team of team leaders? Their track record is what gives them the moral authority to influence the team leaders around them. But in addition to those qualities, three major skills are necessary to excel as a Leader of Leaders. Think of them as the triple A's of leadership.

Advocacy. The Leader of Leaders must be able to advocate for their Team Leaders what they need from upper leadership. This is especially true when allocating limited resources. These teams may need new equipment or more training. During the pandemic in 2020, small groups in our church were unable to meet in person. Each group scrambled, using various platforms and personal equipment to make this happen. After the groups began meeting back on campus, not everyone was comfortable in attendance. Some came in person, while others preferred to remain online. These groups needed a solution for how to manage both groups of people over an extended period of time. The Leader of Leaders communicated these needs to senior leadership. Quickly, equipment was purchased and installed to meet the needs of these groups. This happened quickly because of the advocacy of the Leader of Leaders.

Accountability. The role of the Leader of Leaders is to hold the Team Leaders accountable to goals and outcomes. They are to make sure teams don't go rogue and do whatever they want to do—I have seen firsthand the chaos that ensues when a team is left to its own devices without accountability. Before long, the team can quickly become untethered from the mission of the church and develop its own agenda. This usually breeds conflict and turf wars. All the teams must work together to accomplish the mission of the church, and this requires accountability. Now this accountability can take multiple forms. It certainly involves regular check-ins and reporting. It can include coaching and problem solving. All of this is necessary to ensure everyone pulls in the same direction, but it must be consistent and compassionate.

LEADER OF LEADERS HOLD THE TEAM LEADERS ACCOUNTABLE.

Attraction. The Leader of Leaders must attract leaders under them and develop them. For example, they need to attract Self-Leaders who can engage in the ministry as volunteers. Once they identify these new Self-Leaders, they need to develop them into Team Leaders. They also need to be looking for stellar Team Leaders who are successful and prepare them to move up the pipeline. For example, a guest services coordinator may oversee multiple Team Leaders for a certain worship hour: the coffee Team Leader, the usher Team Leader, the greeter Team Leader, and the parking lot Team Leader. Because they oversee these various Team Leaders, they are a Leader of Leaders. Their job is to help these Team Leaders attract great volunteers and then develop them to be Team Leaders who can grow the ministry.

Let me post a warning here. This can be difficult in a church setting because usually only a few seats are available at this level within a certain department. Only one or two Leaders of Leaders might be in a guest services department or a men's ministry department or an adult groups department. That is why some Leaders of Leaders are reluctant to elevate their best Team Leaders to be Leaders of Leaders. They might think, *If I elevate this Team Leader, he will take my spot! Plus, I will lose my best Team Leader.* That is why Leaders of Leaders need to be shared across the organization. If one operates well in one department, they may be able to move into another department and lead effectively as well. The whole organization needs to be on the hunt for these incredible leaders and develop them.

WARNING INDICATORS

According to *The Leadership Pipeline*, there are three indicators that a Leader of Leaders may be struggling. These behaviors could serve as a warning light on the dash if you begin to see them consistently in your Leader of Leaders. What are they?

If your Leader of Leaders has difficulty delegating to Team Leaders and prefers doing the work themself, that's a warning sign. Just as with the second level of leaders, no longer is this person called to be a doer of the work but a leader of the team that works together. Another warning sign is an inability to communicate clearly to Team Leaders. If Team Leaders are confused, uncertain of their priorities, or just generally unclear about the direction of the ministry, that is a problem. The Leader of Leaders must be a master of clarity and communication. Warning sign number three is a single-minded focus on getting things done. This may sound odd. After all, don't you want someone focused on getting things done? Here is the problem: if the Leader of Leaders is doing that, then they are not developing their Team Leaders. At this stage, the Leader of Leaders focuses more on coaching and developing rather than just pulling off an event or getting the work done. The final warning sign is choosing clones over contributors. When building out their teams, do they choose people like them, or do they choose people who are most qualified? How they build their teams, how they attract and develop emerging leaders, is critical at this level.[36]

This may be a good time to stop and think about the Leaders of Leaders in your organization. How many fit this role? How many more do you need? Who are the successful Team Leaders you could develop into that role? And of those you have in place, do any of them demonstrate these warning signs? If so, work must be done.

HOW JESUS DEVELOPED LEADERS OF LEADERS

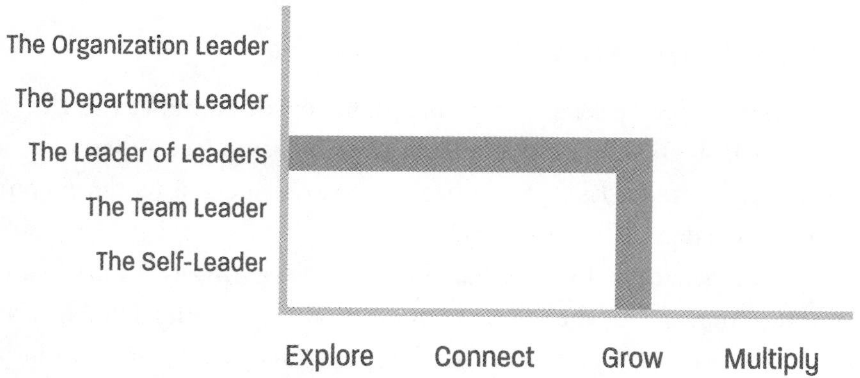

If Jesus cultivated the heart of the leader in the second step of his leadership process, he focused on the hands of the leader in the third. This phase marked the completion of two years of Jesus' earthly ministry and the beginning of the most critical stage of leadership development. Here Jesus spent roughly six months training and equipping his leaders to lead leaders. His training was composed of instruction, demonstration, and modeling.

As I mentioned in Chapter 3, most of Jesus' teaching came from this phase of development. The Sermon on the Mount and the parables all came from this period. Jesus also demonstrated his power over death, disease, and the demonic, showing his followers his power was greater than any other power. Jesus reinforced this truth later after his resurrection: "All authority in heaven and on earth has been given to me" (Matt. 28:18, NIV). And Jesus modeled for his team leaders how to lead, providing them an example to follow. Keep in mind that all the ministry skills Jesus taught his men were cumulative. As leaders move up the pipeline, they continue to add new skills to their leadership toolbelt.

So how did Jesus train Leaders of Leaders?

HELP THEM CHOOSE THE RIGHT TEAM

The ministry was growing, and Jesus sensed it was time to expand his leadership team. Some of these men had been with him from the beginning, and others had joined along the way as Jesus' popularity began to swell. It was time for a change. Luke says Jesus went to the mountain and spent all night in prayer (Luke 6:12). And when day came, Jesus called those men he wanted to him. Mark records it this way:

> Jesus went up the mountain and summoned those he wanted, and they came to him. He appointed twelve, whom he also named apostles, to be with him, to send them out to preach, and to have authority to drive out demons. He appointed the Twelve: To Simon, he gave the name Peter; and to James the son of Zebedee, and to his brother John, he gave the name "Boanerges" (that is, "Sons of Thunder"); Andrew; Philip and Bartholomew; Matthew and Thomas; James the son of Alphaeus, and Thaddaeus; Simon the Zealot, and Judas Iscariot, who also betrayed him. (Mark 3:13–19)

Jesus chose his next level of leaders, naming them "apostles," which means "sent ones." These were the ones he chose to join his school of leadership and to take over the reins of leadership after he was gone. One of the key skills needed by a Leader of Leaders is the ability to choose a leadership team wisely. Back when I was a young ministry leader, all a ministry seemingly needed to be successful was a great band and a charismatic leader. Today it's a different story. You need a whole team of qualified and exceptionally gifted leaders. If you don't have great leaders around you, your ministry will never realize its full potential. You need great leaders. The Leader of Leaders is responsible for identifying, recruiting, and developing Team Leaders who will be successful and eventually move up through the pipeline.

A LEADER OF LEADERS MUST CHOOSE A LEADERSHIP TEAM WISELY.

How do you choose the right leaders? Look at Jesus' example. First, Jesus started in prayer. He carved out significant time to pray over this leadership choice. And I'm sure his prayer to the Father included asking for wisdom and discernment. He wanted to be sure the men he chose were those his Father had already chosen. Choosing the right leaders on your team starts with prayer. Now most leaders would agree with that statement, but few do it. They may kick off a personnel meeting with a customary prayer, but few devote all night to praying over their leadership team. In prayer we don't bend God toward our will; rather, we bend our will toward him. We say things like, "Father, keep me from making a mistake. Keep me from drifting off course from what you want."

You might push back and ask, "Did Jesus make a mistake when he chose Judas to be on his team?" It might look that way, but even the choice of Judas was purposely made and at the Father's direction. John 6:64 tells us, "Jesus knew from the beginning those who did not believe and the one who would betray him." A few verses later we read, "Jesus replied to them, 'Didn't I choose you, the Twelve? Yet one of you is a devil.'" (John 6:70). I believe this was revealed to Jesus as he met with the Father that night. However, despite Judas's eventual betrayal, Jesus still chose Judas to be part of his team and serve in a critical role.

In addition to prayer, Jesus also observed these men. Over the course of months, Jesus had certainly seen their abilities, temperaments, personalities, and potential. He saw Matthew's heart for his unreached friends and how he threw a party just so he could introduce them to Jesus. He saw Peter's bewilderment as he drew in a large catch of fish. He saw James and John's eagerness to leave their family business and follow him. Jesus observed these men marvel after friends lowered a paralyzed man through the roof and he healed him. In all these situations, Jesus took note of their faith and their obedience. Mark says Jesus called "those he wanted." These were the men he knew, observed, and trusted to take this next step of training.

When choosing someone to join your leadership team, you need to take time to observe them. This, of course, is better if you raise leaders up from within your own ministry. Those brought in from the outside can't be observed in a hiring process to the same degree as those you've seen serve faithfully over time. Observation, faithfulness, potential, agreement with your vision—all these characteristics are critical. Using temperament analysis tools and personality indexes may prove helpful, especially for those you don't know as well. We certainly use them. But taking a hard, long look is always best. Develop a comprehensive protocol for making these decisions, especially if it involves hiring someone. Just a simple checklist to be sure all the issues are addressed and all the steps have been taken before a choice is made will keep you from making bad hires that eventually hurt people and your ministry.

As you make staff hires or other leadership moves, do it in collaboration with others. Some on our staff team are masters at interviewing. Others are good at background research. Still others are too optimistic. Submitting to a predetermined process allows the Spirit of God to confirm to multiple people whether a person is a good fit for the team.

HIGHLIGHT INTEGRITY

At every level of leadership, integrity is important. As you ascend the pipeline, and the leader has more and more people under their influence, integrity becomes even more critical. A lack of integrity at that level could be catastrophic to the whole ministry. We have all seen tragic situations where a pastor was dismissed for a lack of integrity, and it took years for the church to recover. That is why, at this level, Jesus gave special attention to integrity.

AT EVERY LEVEL OF LEADERSHIP, INTEGRITY IS IMPORTANT.

Immediately after choosing his twelve apostles, Jesus sat down to teach them. This sermon is known as the Sermon on the Mount. In many ways, it was the ordination sermon for these newly appointed leaders. In it, Jesus covered a variety of issues related to the kingdom of God and how we live in it. But specifically, he addressed the necessity of integrity. He especially pointed out the hypocrisy of the religious leaders' devotion to God in regard to giving, praying, and fasting. Jesus rebuked the religious leaders for doing all three to be seen by men (Matt. 6:1, 5, 16). Outwardly they appeared very devoted, but inwardly they were not.

Later in Jesus' ministry he accused these leaders directly to their faces:

> Woe to you, teachers of the law and Pharisees, you hypocrites! You are like whitewashed tombs, which look beautiful on the outside but on the inside are full of the bones of the dead and everything unclean. In the same way, on the outside you appear to people as righteous but on the inside you are full of hypocrisy and wickedness. (Matt. 23:27–28, NIV)

For Jesus, integrity was paramount. His leaders had to be the same on the outside as they were on the inside. Far too often, spiritual leaders are exposed for playing the hypocrite. This is simply tragic. People don't look for perfection; instead, they look for leaders who are genuine people, with struggles and all.

I recently gathered a few emerging leaders and took them on a five-day retreat to build relationships and cast vision. As we shared our stories of success and loss, victories and failures, hopes and disappointments, these men were galvanized together in mutual respect. They left knowing that pastors and leaders are not perfect people. We are flawed and rely daily on God's grace. That kind of integrity is attractive.

Integrity is the currency of leadership. Once your integrity is gone, you are done. This is especially true in ministry settings because someone serving in Jesus' name represents Jesus and should be completely trustworthy. When lapses of integrity are brushed aside, explained away, or even intentionally kept hidden, the whole church suffers. Consequently, as you raise up Leaders of Leaders, you must evaluate for integrity, talk about integrity, and confront a lack of integrity at every turn. This is why Paul puts integrity as a top qualification for church leadership (1 Tim. 3:1–12). Even a leader's integrity and reputation among people who don't know Jesus is important. Why? Because they represent Jesus and his mission in the world.

PRACTICE CLARITY AND ACCOUNTABILITY

In this phase of training, Jesus deployed his men into the work of the ministry. But he did it in a way that set them up for success, not failure. Instead of using the "sink or swim" method, Jesus intentionally modeled the skills he wanted them to perform, and then he allowed them to try it with accountability. Ultimately, he would release them to teach others. As I mentioned earlier, he used the "watch one, do one, teach one" method. In Luke 8:1 we read, "After this, Jesus traveled about from one town and village to another, proclaiming the good news of the kingdom of God. The Twelve were with him" (NIV). They had certainly seen Jesus do this before, but this time was different. Watching someone else do a task is one thing, but it's quite another to watch so you can do it on your own. And in this season of leadership training, the disciples watched and learned how to lead like Jesus. Notice the four things Jesus gave them that clarified their ministry responsibilities and enhanced accountability.

Jesus gave them clear authority. Luke 9:1–2 says, "When Jesus had called the Twelve together, he gave them power and authority to drive out all demons and to cure diseases, and he sent them out to proclaim the kingdom of God and to heal the sick" (NIV). These men were not going out in their own authority, but in the authority of Jesus. This was a huge moment for these men. They had seen Jesus heal and preach, but they had never done it. Now it was their turn. I'm sure this was an incredible faith builder. Their minds likely swam with thoughts such as, *What if I can't preach as well as Jesus? What if the Spirit of God doesn't heal like with Jesus? What if the people don't accept me like they do Jesus?* This was probably both terrifying and exhilarating at the same time. Yet this was their time to put into practice what they had learned.

Jesus gave them clear credentials. Mark says Jesus sent the men out in pairs (Mark 6:7). While this cut down the number of villages they could cover in a short period of time, it gave them credibility because according to the Old Testament, any judgment had to be verified by two witnesses (Deut. 19:15). The listing of disciples appears in Matthew's account, and it reads as if they traveled in pairs. This is why some have suggested these were the pairs sent out. I wonder who was paired with Judas? (You've got to look this one up yourself in Matthew 10:4.)

Jesus gave them clear instructions. They were to go only to Jewish settlements and villages (Matt. 10:5). They were to preach the coming kingdom (Matt. 10:7). They were to perform miracles (Matt. 10:8). They were not to take money or many supplies—this was a faith-stretching mission (Matt. 10:9–10). When they entered a village, they were to stay where the Lord opened a door, and if no door was open, they were to go to the next village (Matt.10:11–15).

Jesus also gave them clear encouragement. Jesus warned that opposition would come, but the disciples were not to be afraid (Matt. 10:19, 26–31). And as disciples went out, the Spirit of God filled them, and they accomplished great works: "So they went out and preached that people should repent. They drove out many demons, anointed many sick people with oil and healed them" (Mark 6:12–13). Immediately following their mission trip, Jesus pulled his disciples away to be with him and regroup (Matt. 14:13; Mark 6:31–32; Luke 9:10). I'm sure they had incredible moments of hearing stories and celebrating God's power working through them as well as teaching moments as Jesus coached them and prepared them for what was ahead.

As you train up Leaders of Leaders, they need to practice clarity and accountability. Do they know how to give clear instructions to their Team Leaders? Have they modeled for their Team Leaders what to do, how to act, what to say? Are their Team Leaders prepared? Are their questions answered? Is there clarity? Do your Leaders of Leaders know how to hold people accountable? Do they celebrate wins? Do they point out places for improvement? Without clarity, accountability is impossible. And without accountability, the mission will fail.

GRIT

Ministry isn't always easy. In fact, at times you will have to care for others while your own heart is breaking. You will need to comfort others when you need to be comforted. And you'll need grit, endurance, determination. As Angela Duckworth writes, "Enthusiasm is common. Endurance is rare."[37] Leaders of Leaders will surely find themselves in seasons of ministry where the enthusiasm has faded and all that remains is endurance. Jesus modeled for his men this important lesson at this stage in their development.

The men had just finished their first preaching tour, and it was a phenomenal success. The crowds were coming, the ministry was growing, God was moving, and people were being saved. But amid it all, Jesus received terrible news. His dearly loved cousin, John the Baptist, had been killed at the whim of an evil king. I'm sure sorrow flooded Jesus' heart. It was a strange confluence of two realities: on the one hand was excitement and celebration and on the other hand was deep grief and loss.

Jesus needed to pull away with his men, but the crowds kept pressing against them, wanting them. Everywhere they docked their small fishing boat, a crowd awaited them. And even though his heart was heavy, Jesus had compassion on them (Mark 6:34). As day gave way to night and the sun set over Galilee, Jesus took five loaves and two fishes, blessed them and multiplied them, feeding the hungry crowd. He then sent the crowds home satisfied, and his disciples crossed the lake for the night.

Jesus then went to a solitary place on the mountain to be alone with his Father (Matt. 14:23). Eremos Cave sits on the north shore of the Sea of Galilee. The name comes from the Greek word for "solitary and quiet." People can still visit the cave today, and I've been there several times. And every time, I picture Jesus there praying, weeping, and finding comfort in his Father.

The ability to lean on Christ and care for others amid their personal pain is an attribute of godly leaders.

But that doesn't mean leaders don't need a break. I'm not advocating that leaders work nonstop at the sacrifice of their health or families. But sometimes Leaders of Leaders will have to care for others during their own darkest moments. And in those moments, Jesus shows that his grace is sufficient.

CONFRONTING CONFLICT

Jesus certainly wasn't immune to the sting of criticism and conflict. Up to this point, most of the criticisms came from the religious leaders of his day, but now they also came from many who considered themselves disciples of Jesus. Many of the crowds who followed Jesus were there for the miracles alone. His healing power drew large crowds, but when Jesus preached on suffering and solitary allegiance to God and his kingdom, many began to push back.

Jesus had just fed the crowds physical bread, and now he explained that he was the Bread of Life, bringing nourishment to their souls. Just as Moses gave the Israelites bread from heaven, so now the ultimate Bread of Life had come from heaven to give them complete satisfaction: "I am the living bread that came down from heaven. If anyone eats of this bread he will live forever. The bread that I will give for the life of the world is my flesh" (John 6:51). These words were not politically correct, and many of these would-be disciples grumbled and complained, just as their forefathers had done in the wilderness with Moses.

So how did several of the supposed disciples respond? John writes, "Therefore, when many of his disciples heard this, they said, 'This teaching is hard. Who can accept it?'" (John 6:60). It's one thing when grumblers and naysayers come from the outside. That's expected. But when they come from the inside, it hurts. Jesus' own followers were not willing to accept the truth of Jesus' divine identity and eternal mission. They just wanted him to meet their needs and give them pleasant stories and encouraging words.

How did Jesus handle this? He confronted the issue head-on: "'Does this offend you?'" (John 6:61). He didn't avoid the conflict; he welcomed it. He knew a conflict avoided is a conflict that will eventually grow. Leaders of Leaders certainly deal with conflict. While each Team Leader may deal with only a few conflicts, the Leader of Leaders must deal with the various conflicts that rise up from the Team Leaders they manage. This is a huge coaching point. Leaders of Leaders must know how to address issues head-on and not avoid them. They must have hard conversations with grace and respect. They need a proven method to conflict resolution that they can follow and teach to their Team Leaders.

LEADERS OF LEADERS MUST KNOW HOW TO ADDRESS ISSUES HEAD-ON AND NOT AVOID THEM.

After Jesus addressed this grumbling and complaining attitude, many of the would-be disciples abandoned Jesus and refused to follow him anymore (John 6:66). However, those who stayed were even more committed. I've found that to be true in addressing conflict. You hope every conflict can be resolved, and everyone moves forward together. But that is not always the case. Some will choose to stay; some will choose to cut ties and move on. Regardless of people's decisions, the leader's role is to address issues and forge a path toward peace, reconciliation, and hope.

SCALING DOWN

In my mind, the role of the Leader of Leaders is incredibly vital yet inexplicably overlooked in most churches. We need more Leaders of Leaders. We need to identify them, train them, develop them, and release them. This is necessary for a church ministry to grow. One of the main reasons this doesn't happen is because too many Department Leaders want to function as Leaders of Leaders, which I will address more fully in the next chapter. I have seen this time and time again. The Department Leader resists developing this layer of the pipeline because they would rather be more hands-on in doing the work of ministry than leading it. When this happens, the ministry scales down instead of scaling up. As I said earlier, this role is the secret link to growth and expansion.

Let me also make one more comment about spiritual development. Jesus saw this phase of training as developing the skills needed to lead. He trained the disciples on the skills of team building, accountability, and conflict management. He also drove home the vital nature of a leadership integrity that was dependent on the Father. But these skills were predicated upon his previous spiritual training. Jesus had trained them to walk with God through prayer and the Word, to share their faith, and to invest in a few. These spiritual skills were necessary for them to multiply the movement. If that was true in Jesus' ministry, then it should be true in yours. Leaders of Leaders must be fully trained disciples. They should be men and women who have progressed down the disciple-making pathway to the point where they are fully capable of investing spiritually in their Team Leaders and producing multiplying disciples.

All these qualities are necessary for Leaders of Leaders to grow and thrive in your ministry. Are you training your Leaders of Leaders this way? Do you have an intentional plan to identify and develop leaders at this level? Your answer may determine the depth and breadth of your ministry in the future. And once a person proves themselves faithful in leading leaders, then they are ready to lead at one of the highest levels in ministry: the Department Leader.

GROUP DISCUSSION QUESTIONS

1. What is the unique role of the Leader of Leaders in the ministry organization?
2. What are some of the key challenges with this role?
3. In this chapter, I mention three skills that are important for this role. Which of these three A's is most important for your leaders? Why?
4. Why is this level of leadership often underdeveloped in most ministries?
5. What are some next steps you need to take to develop these important leaders in your ministry?

DISCIPLE-MAKING MOVEMENT PROFILE

The West African Movement

Pastor Dion Robert is the lead pastor of the International Baptist Church in the Ivory Coast, West Africa. Today the church is composed of 12,000 small groups encompassing 1,800 congregations throughout West Africa, Europe, Canada, Denmark, Mexico, and the United States.

Pastor Dion, a short-statured, distinguished man with white hair and kind eyes, has led this church to become one of the largest churches in the world, but it didn't start that way. The congregation began with the help of missionaries from the Baptist International Mission Board. A small, makeshift building was built, and a few pews were set up. The missionaries said his job was to fill the pews with people.

Dion had never been a pastor before, and he certainly didn't know what to do, but he was determined to preach, so on Sundays he stood behind his pulpit and preached to the empty pews. He said, "My wife thought I was crazy," but then God gave him a vision, not just of a large church but also of a swelling movement that overflowed the banks of his city and country—a church with a deep and wide international reach. It wasn't long before the church began to grow at a rapid rate.

When asked his secret for the church's explosive growth, Dion gave three answers centered on discipleship. "First," he said, "you must preach obedience to Jesus. This is something people don't want to hear, but the church will never grow if God's people will not obey." In the early days, he had 150 people in the church. When he began to preach obedience, seventy-five people left, but those who stayed became the nucleus of the movement.

Second, he said you must win people to Christ and disciple them. Once a person makes a profession of faith, they are placed in a cell group close to where they live. There this new believer is discipled in the basics of the Christian life: how to read God's Word, how to pray, etc. This cell group is like a mother to a newborn baby. They teach this new believer how to live as a Christian at home, at work, and at church.

After six months of training, the cell group recommends that the new believer be baptized. Following their baptism, the new disciple trains for another six months in his home cell group. They learn how to love God and serve the mission of God. Only after this training are they able to serve in the church. Dion asked, "How can a person lead the church if he is not a disciple? How can a person be an evangelist if he is not first a disciple?"

Last, there is prayer. Every person in a cell group is to pray for someone lost. They are encouraged to lead one person to Christ a week. Dion said, "There are many lost people in our city!" Once a cell grows beyond fifteen people, they multiply to another cell group.

This explains how the church has grown so quickly in the Ivory Coast. In Abidjan, the former capital city, the church has fifty-eight church campuses and over five thousand cell groups. When members move to other cities and countries, they are encouraged not to join another church but to start a church in their city. Over time, this church has multiplied churches all over the world. Pastor Dion is an incredible example of a disciple-making leader who led his church to multiply, and the world is better for it.

9

DEVELOPING DEPARTMENT LEADERS

Sitting in a corporate boardroom can be intimidating because this is where the best and the brightest gather to discuss strategies, assess progress, and make tactical decisions for the business. For several years I served on the board of a local hospital that was part of one of the largest hospital systems in the state of Texas. Around the U-shaped large conference table were senior leaders of the hospital, board members, leaders of various departments within the hospital, and doctors in white coats. Everyone served in a significant role at the hospital. During the meetings, each department leader presented to the board the performance of their department over the previous months. Deficiencies were glaring, and no excuses were accepted. At the end of their presentation, the leaders articulated what action steps they would take to improve their department. I always walked away from those highly charged meetings with a profound respect for those leaders who championed their department and were so fiercely committed to its success.

Department Leaders serve a crucial role in the success of every organization. These are the upfront leaders who set the pace and strategy for moving a whole department of the organization forward. In a business, this person may lead a sales department or manufacturing department. In a hospital, they may run the emergency department or outpatient surgery department. In a church, these are the visible leaders of the students or kids departments, guest services or worship departments, finance or communications departments. The Department Leader's primary purpose is to lead an entire department of the church toward growth and success, giving direction to all Leaders of Leaders, Team Leaders, and Self-Leaders. Because this person is the leader, they wield tremendous influence church-wide, and hundreds of people are impacted by their decisions. These Department Leaders are usually highly skilled, full-time pastors or professionals.

I distinguish here between pastors and professionals only to point out that some of them oversee pastoral ministries such as adults or outreach ministries, while others oversee professional departments such as communications, finance, or facilities. Whatever the case, both are critically necessary, and both should be led by highly trained leaders who have great capacity to grow the organization by growing their department.

THE SEVEN DEADLY SINS OF A DEPARTMENT LEADER

Because Department Leaders are so vital to the ministry and because they are public leaders, much rides on these leaders to be successful. Organization Leaders count on them to perform at a high level; anything less can either hold the ministry back or at worst cause it great harm. Having led these leaders for many years, I've noticed several "sins" of departmental leadership that hold back the church and keep these leaders from reaching their potential.

Leading from Skill, Not Spiritual Maturity. A Department Leader often rises to power quickly because of their natural skill or personality. This leader may be an incredible communicator, visionary, or creative, or just dynamic in their people skills. Maybe they came from a large church and carry with them a "superstar" quality that is nothing short of magnetic. Whatever the case, people are drawn to them. The problem comes when this person may have risen to leadership before they had time to grow in their own spiritual development. Not that they don't know the Lord or don't have a genuine walk with God, but many rising stars become falling stars because they have never been personally discipled. Therefore they do not have a solid grasp of the basic disciplines of the Christian life, and their character has not had time to be tested and proven.

Just as a skier falls when their weight gets over their skis, a leader will surely fall when their talent gets ahead of their character. This is why I propose a new rule:

Never move someone up into leadership who has not first moved down the disciple-making pathway.

You'll be tempted to break this rule. You might be afraid you will lose someone to another church, and that could happen. You might be afraid to offend them by suggesting you want to invest in their personal spiritual growth, or you might just be desperate for help, and this person has a lot to offer. All these are reasons to break the rule. But when you break it, you put everyone at risk. That superstar leader will be hurt because they will soon be leading out of talent and not character, which will result in a fall. Thus, you put the ministry at risk because when a leader falls, people get hurt.

Acting like a Leader of Leaders. There is a difference between being a Department Leader and a Leader of Leaders. Organizationally, the Leader of Leaders is responsible to manage Team Leaders within a department. Their purpose is to solve problems, care for and develop the Team Leaders, and make sure the work is done properly. This is a hands-on kind of ministry role. The Department Leader, however, requires thinking at a higher level. This person is responsible to ensure the whole department heads in the right direction. They are concerned with managing limited resources while growing the ministry and building a dream team. At this level, the Department Leader thinks more about the health of the ministry as a whole, not just one team or individual. It doesn't mean they are not concerned about individuals or don't step into pastoral care opportunities, but the whole department looks to them to set direction and grow the ministry.

However, some Department Leaders want to spend more time leading teams instead of leading the department. They want to do all the counseling. They want to be the one everyone comes to for answers. As a result, they do not raise up many Leaders of Leaders and assume that role themselves. While this sounds noble and even admirable to want to "shepherd" the people in this way, this keeps the department from growing because now everything hinges on one person's ability or personality. Instead of leading to growth, they are now just in the way. This person thinks and behaves more like a Leader of Leaders and not a Department Leader.

To be fair, this is how most ministries begin. Take student ministry as an example. In the early days of ministry, the student pastor often did everything. He led the teams. He recruited all the volunteers. He planned all the events, picked up the food, set up the rooms, and tore everything down after every event. He visited students at school, attended all the ballgames, and counseled parents. He did it all. But as the student ministry began to grow, he was forced to raise up Leaders of Leaders to take over some of those responsibilities so he could take on larger leadership challenges and move the ministry forward. He developed one person to oversee all his small group leaders. He developed another person to oversee his school outreach strategy and another person to oversee the training of parent-focused support groups. Now the student pastor can simply lead the ministry through these appointed Leaders of Leaders. This allows him the time and energy to think about strategy, vision, making good decisions, hiring staff, and measuring success. If a Department Leader is unwilling to release some of the ministry to others, they hold everyone back, including themself.

Not Being a Team Player. Department Leaders think about growing and developing their department. That is their focus. Yet they also work alongside other Department Leaders so the whole church can grow. Student pastors work alongside kids pastors, worship pastors, adult pastors, and outreach pastors. They all lead their individual departments, but they must work together as a team so the whole church can grow. As obvious as it may seem, some Department Leaders forget this piece. They are so transfixed on their department that they forget they are part of a larger team. They can even begin to see other departments as competitors, all wrestling for limited resources, such as budgeted money, calendar space, communication services, and facility requests. They see their ministry as an island unto themselves, an independent team that can operate as it pleases.

This, of course, leads to silos and intra-ministry conflicts. If left unaddressed, this attitude can turn any department into an arrogant cancer that metastasizes throughout the whole church body. A more subtle symptom of this problem is the Department Leader's lack of consideration for how their decisions impact other ministry leaders. To move quickly or get things done, decisions may be made without the knowledge or agreement of other departments, causing confusion and conflict. At this level, every Department Leader must realize they *lead* a team and they are *on* a team. They lead their department, but they are on a churchwide team of Department Leaders who coordinate together to accomplish the mission of the church.

Failure to Build and Manage a Strong Team. It is incumbent on the Department Leader to build a great team and lead it well. They must identify great Team Leaders and move them up to be Leaders of Leaders. They must help the Team Leaders identify, recruit, and train volunteers to be Team Leaders. This Department Leader is the tide that raises all ships. The very force of their example inspires everyone under them to build great teams and develop the next generation of leaders.

However, when a Department Leader fails to do this, it's a problem. The inability to build great teams comes down to either insecurity or a lack of discernment. If a Department Leader is insecure, they might steer clear of recruiting strong leaders onto their team for fear that they will show them up or reveal their leadership flaws. Instead of staffing to their weakness, they exacerbate their weaknesses by hiring people who are just like them. This cloning makes the leader feel better but renders the team ineffective over time. The other cause of poor team development is a lack of discernment. Some Department Leaders struggle with discerning whom they should bring on the team. Instead of recruiting leaders who are the best fit, who have successful track records, and who have been confirmed by others, this leader appoints leaders they like with no real discernment. Again, the consequences are vast.

Department Leaders must have both security and discernment to build a great team. Then once they have them, they must manage them. Clear communication and directives, ongoing support training, evaluations, coaching, planning meetings, accountability for outcomes—all these skills are necessary to optimize a team's performance and bring out the best in each team member.

Mismanaging Resources. As I stated before, the Department Leader thinks about what other leaders down the pipeline don't think about. An example is how to manage limited resources. Every organization must deal with limited resources, and churches are no different. These resources usually pertain to money, time, people, and equipment. A Department Leader must make wise decisions to manage the financial resources under their control. They must also manage their own time, that of their team, and time commitments of their ministry as it relates to coordinating calendar space with other departments. And then there is equipment. The Department Leader must manage the use of facilities, vehicles, technological equipment, etc., to get the work done. Mismanagement of these precious resources can cause tremendous problems. An overspent budget, a failure to follow up on potential volunteers, errors in reserving meeting space or setting up rooms, missed deadlines due to poor use of time—such mistakes make ministry frustrating and undercut a leader's credibility.

Lack of Initiative. When I was in my twenties, I worked under a seasoned executive pastor who used to smile and say, "Craig, be sure you walk fast everywhere you go. When you walk fast, people will say, 'Look how fast he's walking. He must be working hard. Give that man a raise!' But if you walk slow, people will say, 'Look how slow he's walking. He's not working very hard. Get rid of him!'" He was just teasing, but a nugget of truth was there. Leaders need to show initiative.

Initiative can't be coached. It is an inner drive to work, create, act, and then move the ministry forward independently of others. And a Department Leader must exhibit great initiative. They must possess the inner desire and ambition to do what must be done to be successful. When a Department Leader lacks initiative, the whole ministry loses forward motion. Ministries don't come to a stop. They just keep rolling on with business as usual but without innovation, fresh vision, demand for change, or excitement. Over time, volunteers and leaders will step off the team because they simply don't think it's going anywhere.

WHEN A DEPARTMENT LEADER LACKS INITIATIVE, THE WHOLE MINISTRY LOSES FORWARD MOTION.

A leader might lack initiative for many reasons. They might be going through personal struggles that have zapped their energy and clouded their thinking. They might be discouraged, thinking it's not worth it because nothing is ever good enough. They might feel like they are not empowered to make decisions. They might be paralyzed by the fear of failure or distracted with other matters. Whatever the case, it's important for Organization Leaders to identify the cause of a lack of initiative and restore it as soon as possible.

Confusion on Calling. This is a big one. When a person moves to this level of leadership, there must be a clear calling to vocational ministry. I've seen some leaders rise to this level of leadership because of their giftings and passion for Christ, but they were not able to sustain the rigor and demands of the role because they had no clear calling to ministry.

In one sense, we are all called to ministry. The Spirit of God empowers every one of us with certain spiritual gifts for the building up of the body of Christ (1 Cor. 12:7–11). However, a call to pastor and lead is unique to those who serve in those roles. Peter encourages believers, "Make every effort to confirm your calling and election, because if you do these things you will never stumble" (2 Pet. 1:10). While Peter was speaking generally to a salvific call, I believe his encouragement can extend to the calling for pastoral ministry.

How does someone know they are called to ministry? To begin, a calling originates with God. You cannot call yourself, nor can others call you into ministry. It only comes from the Lord. John Newton, author of "Amazing Grace," once said, "None but He who made the world can make a Minister of the Gospel."[38]

Just as Moses was called through a burning bush, Paul was called in a great light, and Samuel was called by an inner voice, God still calls those he desires to shepherd his people.

Here are some questions to ask to determine a genuine call to ministry:

- Is there a strong unabated desire to serve the Lord through vocational ministry (1 Tim. 3:1)?
- Is there a gifting by the Spirit of God for ministry (Eph. 4:11–13)?
- Is there confirmation of your call by others who know you well in the local church (Acts 16:1–2)?
- Is there a clear inner call of Jesus to serve him in this way (John 21:15)?
- Is there a conviction that not following this call would be disobeying Christ (Acts 26:19)?

Ministry leaders who are confused about their call to ministry will lack the conviction to lead and the endurance to stay when circumstances get hard.

Any one of these seven deadly sins can discredit a leader. I've seen it happen more than once. I've seen talented and passionate leaders lose the trust of the people they lead or the trust of senior leadership because they violated these proven principles. And every time I see it, my heart grieves. I've seen leaders discredited because of an arrogant and unteachable attitude. I've seen some step away because they questioned their calling. I've seen some pull out because they failed to rise up to the challenges of leadership, and I've seen others fail for lack of initiative. I'm sure you've seen it too. That's why Organization Leaders must train Department Leaders on how to avoid these deadly sins and rise above them.

HOW JESUS DEVELOPED LEADERS AT THIS STAGE

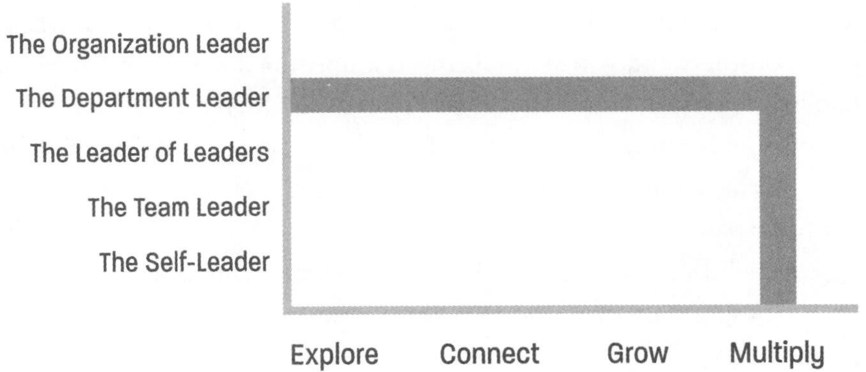

In this final stage of leadership development, Jesus moved his men to multiply. If the early stage was about capturing his shepherding heart and the next stage about mastering the skill of his hands, this stage was about changing the way his disciples thought about people, leadership, and multiplying the movement. This development phase lasted about nine months and led up to Jesus' triumphal entry and subsequent death. So much could be written here about Jesus' approach. The scope of this book is not to exhaust the depths of it. I can only point out a few of the key themes that he seemed to highlight for his leaders before he released them into the world. Organization Leaders would be wise to develop these themes in the Department Leaders they lead, just as Jesus did.

THE MOTIVE

Some of the most difficult words of Jesus are found in this period of his leadership development. Shortly after Peter's confession of Jesus as the Christ, Jesus spoke of the cost that comes with following him. He said, "If anyone comes to me and does not hate his own father and mother, wife and children, brothers and sisters—yes, and even his own life—he cannot be my disciple" (Luke 14:26). Jesus called for complete devotion, even to the point of giving one's life. This kind of commitment was required for the movement to continue.

There comes a time when leadership requires sacrifice. For some today, this sacrifice is very real and very dangerous. As you read these words, brothers and sisters in Christ are imprisoned in North Korea, in indoctrination camps in China, and being slaughtered in West Africa. These believers suffer because they bear the name of Jesus. Here in the West, we have not seen this kind of persecution yet, but there is still a cost to be paid.

Dietrich Bonhoeffer, the great theologian and church leader during the Nazi nightmare of World War II once said:

> The cross is laid on every Christian. The first Christ-suffering which every man must experience is the call to abandon the attachments of this world. It is that dying of the old man which is the result of his encounter with Christ. As we embark upon discipleship we surrender ourselves to Christ in union with his death—we give over our lives to death. Thus it begins; the cross is not the terrible end to an otherwise god-fearing and happy life, but it meets us at the beginning of our communion with Christ. When Christ calls a man, he bids him come and die.[39]

This call to follow Jesus requires a dying to yourself, to your own dreams, desires, and the control you seek over your life. To fully yield yourself completely to Christ. This self-dying is not a one-time act but rather the means by which you find intimacy with Jesus and surrender completely to his will and purpose for your life.

Hard times will come for Department Leaders. They will face resistance, false accusations, and even betrayal. People will let them down. Discouragement can cover them like a dark cloud. And in those moments, the leader must remember their motive for following Jesus in the first place. It must never be for gain or prominence or for self-gratification. It must always be about Jesus. In those moments when they want to quit, when it would be easier to run away from it all, Jesus calls leaders to do the hard things for his name's sake and for his glory. For his movement still changes lives all over the world.

SERVANT LEADERSHIP

When you think of great leadership, what comes to mind? CEOs who started massive corporations? Generals and soldiers who fought battles and won incredible victories? Ministry leaders who started a church from scratch and built it into a sprawling empire? This is certainly how most people define greatness. But not Jesus.

In fact, during this period of Jesus' training, he had to remind his men continually what true greatness was truly all about:

> When he was in the house, he asked them, "What were you arguing about on the road?" But they kept quiet because on the way they had argued about who was the greatest. Sitting down, Jesus called the Twelve and said, "Anyone who wants to be first must be the very last, and the servant of all."
> (Mark 9:33–35, NIV)

True greatness is the opposite of the world's definition. In the eyes of most, true greatness is being first, being served. But Jesus said true greatness is being last and serving others.

Later, during Jesus' last supper with his disciples, we read:

> A dispute also arose among them as to which of them was considered to be greatest. Jesus said to them, "The kings of the Gentiles lord it over them; and those who exercise authority over them call themselves Benefactors. But you are not to be like that. Instead, the greatest among you should be like the youngest, and the one who rules like the one who serves. For who is greater, the one who is at the table or the one who serves? Is it not the one who is at the table? But I am among you as one who serves. You are those who have stood by me in my trials. And I confer on you a kingdom, just as my Father conferred one on me, so that you may eat and drink at my table in my kingdom and sit on thrones, judging the twelve tribes of Israel." (Luke 22:24–30, NIV)

Notice how Jesus contrasted the leadership view of his day with his own. For most people, being great meant being served and sitting at the table. But Jesus had just washed their feet. He had assumed the posture of a servant, and no one was greater than he. True greatness is serving others. It's not found in position or power or recognition but in the humble leadership that is committed to loving like Jesus. This is the kind of leader he will exalt in the world to come.

Department Leaders need to be reminded that true greatness is not a spot on the organizational chart. It's not measured by what meetings you are invited to attend, the size of your office, how many times you speak, or what connections you have. True greatness is serving others with their interests in mind and not your own.

Ken Blanchard states, "As you consider the heart issues of leadership, a primary question you have to ask yourself is, 'Am I a servant leader or a self-serving leader?'"[40] This is a penetrating question that cuts to the motive of ministry. A self-serving leader feels entitled to certain positions and promotions. A self-serving leader is quickly offended when not invited into a decision. A self-serving leader needs to be recognized and publicly rewarded. A self-serving leader quickly leaves when circumstances get difficult.

But a servant leader is quite another thing entirely. This leader sees their position of ministry as an obligation, a trust to hold and protect. And this kind of leader is willing to suffer personally for the benefit of the ministry and the name of Christ. This kind of leader cares more about those they serve than themself. That is the kind of leader Jesus wants.

FORGIVENESS

If you have been in ministry for long, you understand the power of forgiveness. This is one of the themes Jesus reinforces in this period of his leadership training. A leader must be able to endure hardship and forgive others. Why? Because unforgiveness will derail a ministry more quickly than anything I know. Unforgiveness is a cancer that grows with every passing month and consumes its host. Unforgiveness is toxic waste that corrupts everything it touches. Unforgiveness is an unwelcome guest that takes over space in one's heart and mind.

Jesus knew that for his leaders to be successful, they must master and regularly practice forgiveness. This tutorial on forgiveness came on the heels of instruction on church conflict after Jesus instructed his men to follow a prescribed method of resolving interpersonal conflict (Matt. 18:15–18). First, go to the offending person and seek to make things right. If they confess and repent, then all is well. If not, take another person with you and try again. If that doesn't work, keep enlarging the circle of reconciliation until there is either peace or discipline. This is Jesus' plan for restoring conflict in his church.

But Peter still had questions. How many times must he go through this process? How often would he need to forgive repeat offenders? Up to seven times? Jesus replied, "I tell you, not seven times, but seventy-seven times" (Matt. 18:22, NIV). Thus, forgiveness should be limitless. Forgiveness should hold no bounds.

Then Jesus launched into a story about a servant who was forgiven by a good and powerful king of an enormous debt, only to punish without mercy a servant who owed him a month's wage. When the king heard what happened, he threw the wicked servant in jail until his debt was paid in full. Jesus concluded, "This is how my heavenly Father will treat each of you unless you forgive your brother or sister from your heart" (Matt. 18:35, NIV). Does this solemn ending to the story surprise you? In light of all Christ has done in paying our enormous debt of sin, how can we live in unforgiveness to our brother or sister?

SUCH WOUNDS CAN ONLY HEAL WHILE WASHED IN THE WATERS OF FORGIVENESS.

This is important for Department Leaders to grasp because they will deal quite often with conflict, seeking resolution and often suffering wounds in the process. Such wounds can only heal while washed in the waters of forgiveness. And this forgiveness is not so much a punctiliar experience but rather an ongoing commitment to release daily the offenses caused by others and walk in the light of grace and forgiveness, just as Jesus did.

PEOPLE MATTER

How do you see people? Do you judge a person's value by the clothes they wear, their education level, or their social media persona? This world judges by outward appearance, but God looks at the heart. Jesus wanted his men never to forget that every person matters to God. And if every person matters to God, then every person should matter to you too.

This value of Jesus was a stark contrast with the religious leaders of his day. While Jesus taught the crowds, some of these leaders, who thought themselves better than others, chastised Jesus. He saw people not for who they were or what they had done, but for whom God had made them to be. Jesus saw the redemptive potential in everyone he met.

But the religious leaders' hearts were so hard they had lost the ability to see the *imago Dei* implanted in every soul.

In response to this chastisement in Luke 15, Jesus offered three stories: one of a lost sheep, one of a lost coin, and one of a lost son. In each case, something of incredible value was missing. So valuable, in fact, an all-out search was launched to retrieve it. And when it was found, a celebration erupted. When the lost sheep was found, the shepherd rejoiced with his friends. When the woman found her coin, she threw a party. And when the father received his lost son, the whole city came out to celebrate. Jesus said this is how it is in heaven. All of heaven erupts in celebration when just one sinner repents.

Why did Jesus teach this to his leaders? Because Jesus knew our hearts have the terrible tendency to view people wrongly. We often view people from a worldly perspective and not Jesus' perspective. Even Paul agrees with this tendency in us all. He writes, "So from now on we regard no one from a worldly point of view. Though we once regarded Christ in this way, we do so no longer" (2 Cor. 5:16, NIV). Although we used to attach value to a person based on their appearance, position, intellect, athletic achievement, or business savvy, we don't do that any longer. Why? Because all people matter to God. This is the truth that transcends race, gender, class, and nationality: all are valuable in God's eyes and in need of a Savior. And if anyone is in Christ, they are made new again (2 Cor. 5:17). We need to be reminded of this as leaders in ministry today. We need to see people as Jesus sees them, as he sees you and me. Fallen, broken people, in desperate need of God's grace and redemption. That is, after all, why he came.

MULTIPLY THE MOVEMENT

All their training had come to this moment. Think of the Olympic athlete crouching in the blocks awaiting the gun blast. Their mind rewinds to all the early morning runs, all the hours of training, working, sweating, striving. A lifetime of preparation comes down to this one moment. In many ways, this is how the disciples felt. Jesus had trained them for over two years, and now they were released to multiply. All their training was now being tested.

After the Seventy-Two reported to Jesus all they had seen and heard, he replied, "Blessed are the eyes that see what you see. For I tell you that many prophets and kings wanted to see what you see but did not see it, and to hear what you hear but did not hear it" (Luke 10:23–24). These words appear to be a sidebar conversation Jesus had with the Twelve. While they are not mentioned directly in this passage, it makes sense to me that the men who had been trained by Jesus would be leading the way in training the next generation of leaders. Then, after the successful mission, Jesus pulled the Twelve to him and said, "Guys, you are really blessed to be able to see this day. Many kings and prophets of the past wanted to see what you are seeing. Take it all in. This is what it's all about."

Jesus wanted to instill in the hearts of his leaders the imperative of multiplication. Multiplication is not optional; it's not something to be celebrated if we get around to it. Multiplying leaders is the only way to fuel a movement. Department Leaders need to keep the main thing the main thing. That is, sharing the gospel and making disciples who will multiply. In all the whirlwind of events, meetings, luncheons, studies, and productions that crowd our daily schedules, we can easily forget what really matters. Multiplication matters. The movement matters.

Department Leaders must lead the way, just as the Twelve did. They must lead the way by setting an example as they multiply their lives into others. They must lead the way by charting the course of the ministry toward multiplication and movement making. And along the way, they must rejoice like Jesus and marvel that their eyes get to see what so many have longed to see.

DEPARTMENT LEADERS MUST LEAD THE WAY, JUST AS THE TWELVE DID.

Department Leaders are vital to the ministry. They are the faces of their department and, many times, the church. And we desperately need these leaders to be disciple-making leaders. Men and women who walk with

God, reach their world, and invest in a few. High-octane, visionary, passionate leaders who not only lead their departments to grow but also lead toward multiplication and movement building. And the Organization Leaders must invest in these men and women to ensure their success. Organization Leaders must also work hard to create a team atmosphere among these leaders so they don't isolate and compete but collaborate to bring out the best in each other. So much rests on their shoulders, and so much is at stake. No wonder Jesus invested so much in them. Those who excel at this level of leadership are then prepared to take on the most challenging level of ministry leadership: leading the entire organization.

GROUP DISCUSSION QUESTIONS

1. Why are Department Leaders so important to any organization?
2. This chapter mentions seven deadly sins of a Department Leader. Which are most dangerous? Why?
3. What are some of the struggles your Department Leaders face right now?
4. What are some of the ways Jesus taught his leaders to think in this phase of development?
5. What is your biggest takeaway from this chapter?

DISCIPLE-MAKING MOVEMENT PROFILE

The Persian Movement

A disciple-making, church-planting movement is happening today in the Muslim world. More Muslims are coming to faith in Jesus than ever before in recorded history. According to David Garrison, missionary and movement researcher, a movement of Muslims coming to Christ consists of "at least one hundred new church starts or one thousand baptisms that occur over a two-decade period."[41] During Islam's first twelve centuries, no voluntary conversions to the Christian faith occurred. Not until the end of the nineteenth century, that is, twelve and a half centuries after the death of the prophet Mohammed, did voluntary Muslims come to Christ that numbered at least one thousand converts. Garrison contends that such movements taking place in Ethiopia and Indonesia accomplished what no other Christians had been able to do for centuries. By 1965, over two million Indonesians had come to faith in Jesus, and just before the close of the twentieth century, eleven additional movements were identified in the Muslim world. God is doing something new.[42]

One of these movements is taking place in Persia (modern-day Iraq). An Armenian pastor named Seth Yeghnazar (1911–1989) began a Bible study and prayer meeting in his home, which later became a new church plant. One of the men Seth discipled was a young, talented man named Haik Hovsepian Mehr (1945–1994). Mehr, at age twenty-two, was called to serve the Lord in full-time ministry and, years later, was appointed as the National Bishop of the Assemblies of God churches in Iran. As the Ayatollah Khomeini began to pressure Christians, restricting their ability to evangelize, Mehr boldly defied the regime, claiming he was willing to go to jail, or even die, for his faith. Mehr also publicly denounced the mistreatment of Christians imprisoned for their faith and called for their release. On January 19, 1994, Mehr was abducted in Tehran, and ten days later his tortured body was found with multiple stab wounds to the heart. Instead of stifling the Christian movement, Mehr's death only fueled it as Iranian believers grew bolder in their faith and shared the gospel with greater power.

Today Iranian believers continue to share the gospel and personally make disciples who multiply. Prior to the Islamic Revolution, fewer than five hundred Muslims had converted to Christianity in a nation of forty million. Today, hundreds of thousands of Iranians have placed their faith in Jesus Christ.[43]

10

DEVELOPING ORGANIZATION LEADERS

The past seven years had been a whirlwind experience. In that time, I completed my initial seminary training, served in various roles in a large suburban church in Texas, and began to hone my growing leadership skills. Also, during that time, my wife and I had birthed and buried triplets who were born ten weeks premature. A year later, God blessed us with another baby girl. Those seven years were an intensive training process, testing the limits of our faith, and establishing our confidence in the Lord. One thing for sure, I had a calling to be a senior pastor, and now that time had come.

Our small family of three moved from Texas to Oklahoma to lead a stable and loving congregation. The church was what you would expect a church to look like from all outward appearances: red bricks, white Corinthian columns, stained-glass windows, a sky-piercing steeple that stood like a beacon of light to the ever-changing neighborhood. The church had had its years of growth, which had risen on the wave of suburban sprawl as people moved out of the downtown area. Now that wave had moved to the outer ring of the city, leaving this neighborhood to wrestle with the complex challenges of decline and gentrification.

My parents came to help us settle in, and I gave them a tour of my new office, which was a simple room with a small desk and office chair and couch. Seeing the leather chair behind the desk, my mother smiled with pride and commented, "There is the chair of the pastor."

To which I replied, "Yes, and it carries a great weight."

THE WEIGHT

Organizational leadership carries a great weight. Everything rises or falls on leadership, which means the health and direction of a ministry rise and fall on Organization Leaders. These leaders set the vision for the organization. They establish the culture, sometimes even transforming it when it has become toxic and unhealthy. Organization Leaders build the team, make high-stakes decisions that can push the ministry forward or backward, and ensure ministry directives are executed and the financial resources exist to bring those directives to reality. In addition, these leaders must be compassionate pastors, powerful preachers, avid disciple makers, pristine moral examples, effective managers, and godly men of prayer. It's a tall order for anyone. The expectations are high, and the weight is great.

ORGANIZATIONAL LEADERSHIP CARRIES A GREAT WEIGHT.

Organizational leadership in a church looks different in various contexts. For most churches, the senior pastor certainly fits this role. Depending on your ecclesiastical framework, it may also include elders, a board of directors, a leadership or church council, or even executive pastors. The Organization Leader is often a paid staff member with the responsibility to oversee multiple Department Leaders and prayerfully champion the culture of the church through visionary and strategic leadership. While this leader's direct reports may be few, his influence permeates the entire organization and beyond. He is, in many respects, the primary face of the ministry, and his reputation is invariably linked to the organization itself.

WHAT MAKES A GREAT ORGANIZATION LEADER?

Business leaders Charan, Drodder, and Noel offer three insightful questions to assess the effectiveness of Organization Leaders:

- Can these leaders make good decisions that help their Department Leaders and the overall organization succeed?
- Can they work with direct reports to grow them as leaders?
- Can they assess the strategies of Department Leaders in light of the whole organization?[44]

Let's take a closer look at each one of these questions. First, can the Organization Leader make good decisions to help everyone win? As a leader of the entire enterprise, their decision making is critical. These leaders have proven themselves at the departmental level. They know how to grow a department. Now they must oversee several Department Leaders and make wise decisions to help those leaders work together in an optimal way. This is why I advocate for senior leadership teams.

One executive pastor or senior pastor overseeing a large number of Department Leaders is unwise and at the very least inefficient because of decision-making responsibilities. Often an executive pastor is assigned to manage the church so the senior pastor can focus on pastoring and preaching, which leads to one executive pastor overseeing eight to fifteen various Department Leaders. This structure invariably leads to frustration and slows down the ministry. Why? Because rarely does a senior leader have the bandwidth to lead a large group of Department Leaders and help them make wise decisions about their ministries, coordinate the complexities of these various departments, and pull them together into a coordinated team. In most cases, Department Leaders wait in line for decisions to be made so they can execute their ministry plans.

When decisions aren't made quickly, these leaders either stop and wait for a decision, slowing down the ministry, or charge forward without approval, preferring to ask forgiveness rather than permission. Either option is bad. When a church employs a senior leadership team, multiple Organization Leaders oversee a handful of Department Leaders. This allows the Organization Leaders to make decisions quickly and be more responsive to the Department Leaders under their care. It also allows the Organization Leaders to collaborate through challenging issues as a team and come to a consensus. Good, quick decision making is critical at the senior level.

Second, can the Organization Leader develop his Department Leaders in such a way that they can step into senior leadership roles in the future? This development step is critical and often overlooked in ministry settings. Developing leaders at this level relies predominantly on coaching feedback. The Organization Leader must observe his leaders and become intimately acquainted with their strategies, operations, goals, and sticking points. Based on that kind of observation, he can then coach them up to success.

Coaching feedback is vital because it teaches the Department Leaders not just what to *do* but how to *think*, how to anticipate unintended consequences, and how to think multiple steps ahead. This kind of strategic thinking is vital in the role of an Organization Leader. The leaders must not merely impose their plans on the Department Leaders underneath them; instead, through coaching and problem solving, they must help them come to the best conclusions themselves. Setting times of instruction, observation, feedback, and problem solving is necessary to develop Department Leaders and prepare them for their next steps.

Third, can this Organization Leader take the priorities of the whole ministry and implement them into each department, which in turn moves them deeper into the organization, causing the whole ministry to work together as a team? In my experience, this happens as leaders assess the health of the organization and identify key areas for the ministry that must be addressed over the next twelve to eighteen months.

They then present strategies to the Department Leaders, who in turn customize these plans to fit their own departments. This process allows the whole organization to move together in a coordinated effort, instead of acting as a collection of independent ministries. The Organization Leader's responsibility is to facilitate this cooperation. If a Department Leader goes rogue and acts independently of the overall priorities of the church, the Organization Leader must hold them accountable to previously agreed upon guidelines, rules, and policies of the organization.

Identifying key strategies is also important when it comes to distributing resources. If the Department Leader wants to spend money or volunteer man hours on initiatives that don't contribute to the overall forward motion of the church, the Organization Leader may not approve such expenditures or may redirect the Department Leader to align their strategies with the church's overall vision. This can be challenging at times, especially when the overall direction of the ministry appears to conflict with individual department goals. Here the Organization Leader must lead all departments to work toward the collective good.

LETTING GO

Perhaps what defines a great Organization Leader is not as much what he does, but what he chooses not to do. At this level, he must eliminate what made him successful in the past and identify priorities that will make him successful in his new role. For example, an Organization Leader must let go of the urge to act like a Department Leader. As I stated earlier, the Department Leader is a very public role that comes with perks. People know them, they are an upfront communicator, and they are the face of a department. However, the Organization Leader often works behind the scenes, dealing with strategy, evaluation, and leadership issues. A senior pastor who neglects these matters neglects his primary work as the leader of the organization. That doesn't mean the pastor isn't accessible or doesn't care for the people, but his primary duty is to do what no one on his staff can do, which is lead the whole ministry organization.

In addition, the Organization Leader will many times deal with difficult problems that cannot be solved on the ground floor. This will entice him to start thinking and acting more like a Department Leader, becoming engaged on the ground floor with special events and decisions rather than offering his leadership from the thirty-thousand-foot view. He must continually pull up, climb higher, dream bigger, and look further than the people he leads.

Organization Leaders must also let go of the tendency to repeat the strategies of the past and instead embrace creativity, risk-taking, and innovation. He should constantly ask the questions, *Where are our new opportunities for growth? What have we not tried that we should try? How can we ensure we are relevant and effective ten to fifteen years from now? What is happening in our world that we need to address? What are industry trends on which we need to capitalize?* While most leaders in the organization live in the present, the Organization Leader lives in the future. He must look at the organization with unfiltered eyes to see its weaknesses, its hindrances, and its yet-to-be-realized future potential.

The Organization Leader must also resist the urge to fixate only on the pressing weekly demands of ministry and instead cultivate the culture of the organization. A seasoned leader once told me, "Posting core values on a wall doesn't really accomplish much because everyone knows the core values of the organization are found in the senior leader's behavior." What an Organization Leader does lets you know his values. On the flip side, what he doesn't do—what he will not tolerate—also speaks to his values.

Organization Leaders set the culture, and if the goal is to create a healthy disciple-making culture, then the leaders running the organization must embody that culture in the way they live. They also must define the culture continuously. This happens most effectively through storytelling and celebration. When Organization Leaders tell stories of and publicly celebrate behavior that demonstrates their culture, they reinforce

ORGANIZATION LEADERS SET THE CULTURE.

their culture. In this way, these leaders champion the culture they create so it becomes expected throughout the organization and anything other is foreign.

HOW DID JESUS DEVELOP HIS ORGANIZATION LEADERS?

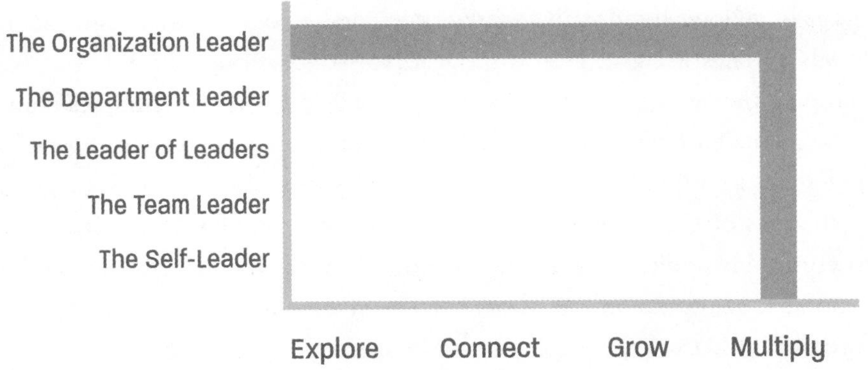

Jesus' last stage of development came in his final days. The movement had begun. He had trained the twelve disciples, and now they had trained others. Multiplication had now reached the fourth generation: Jesus, the Twelve, the Seventy-Two, and those reached by their testimony. Now Jesus' focus was on the cross.

In his final week on earth, Jesus taught in the temple courts to packed crowds that were there in preparation for the Passover. At night he slept outside on the Mount of Olives. In many ways, this week was filled with conflict and confrontations. Some of his harshest words for the religious leaders boiled over this week. However, it was also a tender week with his disciples, as he loved them and poured into them his vision of the future and how they should live.

As I mentioned earlier, in Jesus' leadership training he worked initially to transform their hearts to be that of shepherds, and then he transformed their hands, honing their skills as disciple makers. Next, he transformed their minds, training them to think as he thought about people and their mission. But in this last phase, Jesus transformed their vision, to see how their lives could set in motion a movement that would change the world.

LIVE EXPECTANTLY

As the sun set over the Temple Mount, the limestone pillars turned a shade of yellowish red, and shadows stretched across the stone pavement. It was a majestic sight. Herod spent forty-six years building the massive complex that was a wonder to behold in that day. As the disciples commented on its beauty, Jesus predicted that soon not one stone would be left on another. This caused the disciples to ask what would happen at the end of time. As night surrounded them, Jesus told of what was to come. He spoke of wars and rumors of wars, persecution, and false prophets. He spoke of the abomination of desolation, which had been foretold by Daniel the prophet, that would take place in this very temple with a great tribulation to follow.

Then he said:

> Immediately after the distress of those days, the sun will be darkened, and the moon will not shed its light; the stars will fall from the sky, and the powers of the heavens will be shaken. Then the sign of the Son of Man will appear in the sky, and then all the peoples of the earth will mourn; and they will see the Son of Man coming on the clouds of heaven with power and great glory. He will send out his angels with a loud trumpet, and they will gather his elect from the four winds, from one end of the sky to the other. (Matt. 24:29–31)

I'm sure you could have heard a pin drop. Every eye was fixed on Jesus as their minds raced.

When would this happen? Jesus said no one knows, only the Father. "Therefore be alert, since you don't know what day your Lord is coming"

(Matt. 24:42). Alert. Expectant. Faithful. This is how Jesus wanted his disciples to live every day, to go about their mission knowing their time was short and his coming was soon.

Jesus underscored this attitude in Matthew 25 when he talked about a master who left on a journey and entrusted talents to his servants to invest. To one servant he gave five talents, to another two talents, and to another one talent. When the master returned, he called his servants in to see what they had done with the talents. Two servants had worked hard to double the master's money and were greatly rewarded, but one did nothing and hid the money in the ground. Why did Jesus tell them this story? The parable is sandwiched between the parable of the ten virgins and the teaching of the sheep and goats to emphasize Jesus' insistence that disciples live with a sense of expectancy for his return.

This is incredibly important for Organization Leaders. We must be constantly reminded that the reason we serve the Lord is in response to Jesus' command to make disciples to the ends of the earth. We must put the work we are doing into the context of eternity, doing it faithfully because he is coming soon. We do not serve Jesus for the praise of others, only for the praise of heaven. Our reward is not in this world but in the one to come.

ABIDE IN CHRIST

From the upper room, it is not a long walk down the southwestern steps of Jerusalem across the Kidron Valley to the small garden of Gethsemane. The name of the place means "olive press." Still today ancient olive trees are there, some twisted and aged with time, that have lived for hundreds of years and continue to produce fruit. I imagine there was also a small vineyard along that stretch of space on the side of the Mount of Olives. As Jesus and his men passed through on their moonlit walk, he stopped. Taking a cluster of grapes in his hands, he began teaching them one more lesson:

> I am the true vine, and my Father is the gardener. Every branch in me that does not produce fruit he removes, and he prunes every branch that produces fruit so that it will produce more fruit. You are already clean because of the word I have spoken to you. Remain in me, and I in you. Just as a branch is unable to produce fruit by itself unless it remains on the vine, neither can you unless you remain in me. I am the vine; you are the branches. The one who remains in me and I in him produces much fruit, because you can do nothing without me. (John 15:1–5)

Just as a branch cannot bear fruit apart from the vine, Jesus' disciples could not bear lasting eternal fruit apart from him. Jesus' exhortation was to "remain." The word means "to abide, to make your home with, to be intimately connected to someone or something." By remaining in Christ, one bears "much fruit," and nothing can be done of any eternal significance without remaining in Jesus.

Remaining in Jesus is critical for leadership at any level, but most certainly for Organization Leaders. The demands of the job, the pressure it provides, and the weight of decisions can be overwhelming and suffocating to your spiritual walk with Jesus. There will always be work to be done. There will always be conflict to resolve. There will always be strategies to form, plans to execute, people to care for, and projects to be completed. The grind of the work can wear down the strongest soul. That is why Jesus said, "Remain in me." Let your mind, heart, and soul find rest in Jesus.

Cultivating an intimate walk with Christ is important not only for the leader's health but also for the health of those he leads.

If Jesus' warning is true that apart from him we cannot do anything significant, then leading others while apart from Jesus is an exercise in futility. A congregation wants to know its Organization Leaders hear from God and walk with Christ. This should inspire Organization Leaders to hold each other accountable in their daily time with the Lord. It should encourage them to take a day monthly to retreat and reflect and hear from God. Jesus' promise of greater fruit should inspire everyone to know him more intimately as they see him work in powerful ways.

SPIRIT DEPENDENCE

As Jesus talked about his departure, the disciples' faces fell. Jesus could see the despair creeping into their hearts. For over three years he had been with them. He had trained them and protected them, but now he was going away. In these final hours he pointed his disciples to their only source of strength. They would not be able to do this work in their own power. They needed the power of God's Spirit.

> Nevertheless, I am telling you the truth. It is for your benefit that I go away, because if I don't go away the Counselor will not come to you. If I go, I will send him to you. When he comes, he will convict the world about sin, righteousness, and judgment: About sin, because they do not believe in me; about righteousness, because I am going to the Father and you will no longer see me; and about judgment, because the ruler of this world has been judged. I still have many things to tell you, but you can't bear them now. When the Spirit of truth comes, he will guide you into all the truth. For he will not speak on his own, but he will speak whatever he hears. He will also declare to you what is to come. He will glorify me, because he will take from what is mine and declare it to you. (John 16:7–14)

Spirit dependence is absolutely required for effective ministry because ministry is a Spirit-empowered enterprise. You can't make someone grow spiritually any more than a farmer can make a crop grow; rather, only the Spirit brings conviction of sin and a desire to turn to Christ. He draws us to Christ (John 6:44), gives us new life (John 3:5–8), makes us new on the inside (2 Thess. 2:13), and places us in God's family (1 Cor. 12:13). Once we come to faith in Jesus, the Spirit lives within us (Rom. 8:9–11) and takes up residence (1 Cor. 6:19–20). He leads us (Rom. 8:4), comforts us (John 14:16), teaches us (John 14:26), and grows us to look more and more like Jesus (Titus 3:5–7).

If any lasting ministry is to be done, it will be done by the work of the Holy Spirit. Just as those early disciples needed God's Spirit to move in power, we need the same today. When Organization Leaders try to move the ministry forward in their own strength, the result is frustration and fruitless ministry. Leaders must huddle in prayer to listen to the Spirit's lead—to discern together where he is at work and how to join in his work.

MOVE PAST FAILURE

Peter was all in. If anyone was going to fail Jesus, it certainly was not going to be him. After all, Jesus had given him the nickname "the rock." Peter was impetuous and fearless. He was a born leader and the oldest of the Twelve. Yet in their final meal together, Jesus predicted that Peter would deny him: "Truly I tell you, . . . tonight, before the rooster crows, you will deny me three times" (Matt. 26:34). I'm sure Peter thought, *That will never happen. I'm the leader, the rock. It's not going to be me.*

But as the night wore on, a dark gloom came over the men. Jesus, overwhelmed with grief and emotion, went a short distance alone to pray. Peter, James, and John were within a few feet of him, but they couldn't keep their eyes open. Suddenly they were awakened by a large squadron of soldiers, a few of the religious leaders, and Judas, one of their own, confronting Jesus.

Peter jumped to his feet, drawing his sword to fight. Soldiers call it the fog of war—moments of sheer chaos and confusion when adrenaline overtakes reason. Peter swung his sword and severed a servant's ear.

Then Jesus commanded Peter to put away his sword as Jesus restored the servant's ear. With that, the battalion collapsed on Jesus, tying him with cords and chains, dragging him away to the house of the high priest. All that night Jesus was interrogated as soldiers beat him and religious leaders falsely accused him, desperately seeking some cause to put him to death.

During this time, Peter and John made their way into the courtyard of the high priest and warmed themselves by the fire, pondering their next move.

A young woman recognized Peter as one of Jesus' followers. "You are one of them."

Peter said, "I don't know what you are talking about."

Later, another young woman said, "This man was with Jesus, the Nazarene!"

Peter's heart pounded. "I don't even know him!"

As people drew closer, they said, "Yes, you are one of them. Your accent gives you away."

Peter cursed and exclaimed, "I tell you. I don't know him!"

Immediately the rooster crowed, and Peter remembered Jesus' words.

Today a church commemorates where Peter's denial took place. On top of the church is a weathervane in the shape of a rooster. Sculptures of Peter and a young woman by a fire tell the story. For us it is ancient history, but for Peter it was devastating. The Scriptures report that Peter ran away and wept bitterly.

Failure in ministry can be crushing. It may be a performance failure where a church dissolved, leaders left, or a church plant failed. Perhaps a congregation lost confidence, or a friend betrayed a trust. Moral failures, family struggles, or emotional problems have forced some to step away from ministry for a season—and others altogether.

Peter's crushing failure was compounded by the fact that he had let Jesus down when Jesus needed Peter the most. Yet on the other side of his greatest failures were Peter's greatest moments. Peter's preaching at Pentecost, the birth of the church, his message to Cornelius, the spread of the movement, his letters to the churches—all of this took place *after* Peter's dismal failure that night. What made the difference?

One of the post-resurrection appearances of Jesus took place on the northern shore in Galilee. Peter and his men were fishing when Jesus called from the shore for them to throw their nets on the other side of the boat. When they did, the net nearly ripped from the great catch! Peter knew it was Jesus. Throwing on his outer coat, he jumped in the water and swam ashore.

There was Jesus, cooking fish over hot coals for breakfast. He looked at Peter and asked, "Peter, do you love me?"

"Of course, I love you," Peter replied.

"Then feed my sheep."

Three times Jesus asked the question, and three times Peter replied. Three times Jesus called him to shepherd his people. Three times—once for every denial. "Follow me," were Jesus' final words on the subject.

Failure is never final. Failure is a moment in time. It is a learning moment for sure, sometimes a life-changing moment, but only a moment. The rest of life stretches past that moment of failure. And that stretch of life is what concerns Jesus the most. Your greatest opportunities for growth, for love, and influence are along that road. Facing your failures and surrendering to Jesus is a lifelong journey. There is no life untouched by failure. There are no leaders who have never failed, and I'm glad. Because in our failures we learn, we grow, and we depend on Jesus even more.

COMMITMENT TO THE MISSION

Paul says Jesus appeared to over five hundred disciples at one time after his resurrection (1 Cor. 15:6). This certainly counts as one of the "many convincing proofs" Luke refers to in Acts 1:3. It is one thing to have the testimony of one or two claiming they had seen the resurrected Christ (perhaps they could have been mistaken), but how could five hundred people all witness the same moment and be wrong? Paul later says many of the witnesses to this great event were still alive and would gladly testify to what they had seen and heard. It is my conviction that this appearance of Jesus was the very same occasion described in Matthew 28:18–20 when Jesus gave his disciples the Great Commission challenge to make disciples of all nations.

If this is true, then it underscores the important fact that the visionary charge Jesus gave on the mountain was not just for the Twelve but the crowd of Christ followers that numbered more than five hundred. Thus, the commission to make disciples of all nations is for *all* believers. And just so there was no question, Jesus added, "I am with you always, to the end of the age" (Matt. 28:20). To whom did he make this promise? Certainly not just the Twelve. They would not live "to the end of the age." He made it to all believers, even those who will be alive when he returns. This Great Commission is not just for the elite and privileged or pastors and missionaries. It is for all who claim the name of Christ. And Jesus left this commission to his leaders to carry out until he comes.

Organization Leaders must never forget what Jesus called his church to accomplish. The expectation of Jesus is not only to increase membership or Sunday morning attendance. The expectation of Jesus is not just to provide creative experiences or relevant worship music. The expectation is not merely to gather people in community, care for the poor, visit the sick, pray for the hurting—although these actions are important. Jesus expects his church to make disciples who will in turn make disciples of all nations until his return. The Organization Leaders' responsibility is to keep that vision front and center. To champion it, celebrate it, fight for it, and give their lives in obedience to it.

THE ORGANIZATION LEADER'S ROLE IS TO RAISE UP AND DEVELOP EMERGING LEADERS.

LEADING EMERGING LEADERS

The Organization Leader's role is to raise up and develop emerging leaders. In my opinion, this responsibility cannot be delegated. While some pastors serve only in the role of teaching and not leadership, those who serve in an organizational leadership role must take seriously their call to develop the leaders around them. This involves clarifying for these leaders the core mission and values of the organization. In addition, he should be sure these leaders are focused on executing agreed upon short-term goals, while lifting their vision to understand the long-term vision of the organization for the next three to ten years. And he should regularly assess their performance in areas such as developing their Department Leaders, assessing departmental strategies, uncovering new growth opportunities, and carrying out organizational initiatives through every level of the organization. To do this, Organization Leaders should devote a significant amount of time to these tasks. While sermon preparation and pastoral matters may take up 40 percent of their time, the remaining 60 percent should be allotted for developing leaders, evaluating strategies, and discovering new opportunities for growth.

Organization Leaders are indispensable. They set the pace, champion the church's culture, build teams, cast vision, set priorities, craft strategies, coach staff, create accountability structures, and ultimately, evaluate the church's success. Their responsibility is a heavy weight for sure. That is why Jesus trained his men not to depend on their own strength or abilities but to depend on him. For Jesus' leaders to be successful long term, they needed to abide in him daily and rely on the Spirit's leadership. They needed to keep their eyes focused on eternity and live with a sense of urgency and expectancy. They needed to be resilient in the face of personal failures and keep the mission front and center in their ministries. And they needed to invest continually in the next generation of leaders so the movement could thrive from generation to generation. These are the kinds of leaders Jesus used to change the world. And these are the kinds of leaders Jesus still uses today.

Jesus was a disciple maker and a movement builder. He made disciples who multiplied, and he raised up leaders who built a movement that continues still to this day. So far, we looked at the discipleship pathway as Jesus' strategic plan for making disciples. We also studied the leadership pipeline and how Jesus developed leaders at every level of his ministry. In this next chapter you will see how these strategies work together to produce exponential growth in the life of your church.

GROUP DISCUSSION QUESTIONS

1. What is the primary purpose of Organization Leaders?
2. What are the three basic skills a good Organization Leader must possess?
3. How would you assess your Organization Leaders (both staff and high-value volunteers, such as elders, church council, etc.)?
4. What did Jesus prioritize in training his Organization Leaders?
5. What are the most challenging aspects of being an Organization Leader?

11

DON'T MAINTAIN, MULTIPLY

Pastor Henri was born in Burkina Faso, a small country bordered by Ghana and the Ivory Coast to the south and Mali to the north. It remains part of the world once dominated by French control, and now it's a self-governing democracy struggling to modernize and grow. The last vestige of the French influence is the language. Most of the educated in the city speak French, while various indigenous languages continue their hold in the remote villages.

Burkina Faso's internal struggle against Islamic terrorists is no secret. In 2016, the death of an American missionary at the hands of terrorists made worldwide news. This spark of violence was by no means an isolated event. While most Muslims in the country are not violent, radical terrorists kill indiscriminately to maintain their dominance in certain parts of the region. Pastor Henri knows this full well. He grew up in Burkina to a father who was a professing Roman Catholic. He grew up going to church, even participating as an altar boy in his younger years, but as he grew older, the God of his father grew more distant. Not until Henri received an opportunity to get his master's degree in the United States did his life change.

While studying at the University of Auburn, Henri was befriended by a man who invited him to church. Henri said, "I remember going into the church building for the first time. Written on the wall were the words 'Jesus is the Light of the World.' That had an impact on me."

He bought a Bible and began to read it as God continued to work on his heart.

Henri later received Christ as his Savior and was personally discipled by an older retired pastor from Haiti who loved God's Word. Henri remembers, "He would sit with me and read the Bible, explaining it to me. Sometimes he would pause for a moment too long, and I knew he had fallen asleep, but after a moment he would wake up and continue. This man taught me God's Word. He discipled me."

Returning to Burkina, Henri plugged into a local church and committed to serving the Lord there. Sometime later, the church announced a leadership change. They had prepared a young man to take over the leadership as pastor. As Henri and others gathered around the man to pray, the elders of the church sensed something was wrong. They asked this young man and Henri to step out of the room while they prayed. Bringing the two back in, they said, "The Spirit has made it clear to us that Henri is to be the pastor of this church." It was a surprise to him, for sure, but clearly God was moving.

Today Henri not only serves as a faithful pastor in the city of Ouagadougou, but he also coordinates all the work of the evangelical church across the entire country. In many ways, Henri is the face of the gospel there. Under his leadership, God continues to raise up churches who are committed to taking the gospel to the villages where many have no gospel witness at all. The plan is quite simple. A church planter from an established church will go to the village and share the gospel. Many will come to faith in Christ, and then they will plant a church there.

"We are committed to discipleship," Henri said. "Once we have a new believer, we don't leave them alone. First, we teach them to pray to God. Then we teach them to read the Bible and obey it in every part of life. We want them to make Jesus the center of their lives." This disciple-making process is the work of the church planter. Once a church is established, then that new church can go to another neighboring village to plant a church there. It sounds simple, but the plan comes with a cost.

We sent a team from our church to help Henri train church planters in Burkina just before the global pandemic shut down travel. Planters from across the country gathered for a week of in-depth prayer and equipping. At the end, everyone pressed in for a photo. Men and women squeezed together shoulder to shoulder, three lines deep, their smiling faces bright with hope and excitement. Yet they face real dangers in the villages. A recent terrorist attack in the northern village of Solhan left 160 villagers dead. The UN continues to condemn the attacks and calls for more security in the remote parts of the country.[45]

But these attacks do not intimidate Henri or these church planters.

They know the risks, but they also know the urgency of the hour and the Great Commission.

Today, Pastor Henri leads the charge for the churches of Burkina to plant 2,400 churches in the villages over the next four years. The plan is ambitious but attainable. "If our established churches would each just plant one church, we could reach this goal in one month." Henri said. "But many of our pastors think their job is only to pastor their church, not to multiply and plant other churches. They are thinking inward, not outward. What we need are more leaders who will make disciples and plant churches." Henri leads a disciple-making movement that will shape the face of his country and its leadership for decades to come. But for that movement to become reality, it will require him to build disciple-making leaders today.

Over the course of this book, I've pushed forward the idea that the church needs disciple-making leaders today. Leaders who lead out of the overflow of their walk with Christ, intentionally investing in others to produce genuine disciples and multiply a movement. We need disciple-making leaders like Pastor Henri and those he has trained who put their lives on the line to advance God's kingdom in their country.

Unfortunately in America, we have many pastors, such as those Henri described in his country, who are fixated on growing their church with little concern for the greater kingdom of God. This sounds harsh, but when you consider that 95 percent of churches never plant another church or have any plans to multiply, it's true. This lack of kingdom engagement isn't the result of church members who are resistant to a God-exalting vision or are unwilling to sacrifice to be a part of something bigger than themselves. The problem lies at the feet of pastors and ministry leaders who do not have a disciple-making DNA and have lost Jesus' vision for building a movement.

MADE TO MULTIPLY

At the core of a disciple-making leader is the intrinsic drive to multiply. Superstar pastors fixate on attraction and retention. They think, *How can I attract more people and keep them so my church will grow numerically?* But the disciple-making pastor is different. He is more concerned with investment and release. He thinks, *How can I invest in more leaders and release them to multiply more churches and expand God's kingdom?* The disciple-making pastor is driven to multiply, and for good reason.

Truthfully, it was a miracle when my girls were born. Early on, Liz and I didn't think we could have children. Multiple trips to the doctor for tests, multiple failed pregnancies, and the loss of triplets took a toll on both of us. But one day she came to me with a pregnancy test stick in her hand. It was positive. We were going to have a baby! Our second daughter came along just a few years later.

Nothing is like having a child. Still today I am blown away by how much they are a mix of Liz and myself. One has her face but my skin tone. The other has her hair but my sense of humor. That God can cause two people to produce another person that is so unique yet so similar to both parents is amazing.

Recently, I found something in Genesis I had never noticed before:

> So God created man in his own image, in the image of God he created him; male and female he created them. And God blessed them. And God said to them, "Be fruitful and multiply and fill the earth and subdue it." (Gen. 1:27–28, ESV)

What stood out to me was that this was the first command God gave the first people on earth: to be fruitful, to multiply, to fill the earth. By the way, this same command was repeated to Noah following the flood (Gen. 9:1). Multiplying your life is a command from God. Reproducing your life is essential to sustaining life. Multiplying your life brings joy, happiness, fulfillment, and purpose. Animals reproduce. Plants reproduce. Everything that is healthy and living multiplies.

Not long ago I was raking up leaves in my yard and picking up acorns that had fallen from the tree. There were hundreds of them. But I noticed some had already made their way underground and started to sprout roots. I saw a shoot coming up out of the ground, and it hit me, *This tree is doing everything it can to reproduce!*

The same is true in our spiritual lives. Healthy things reproduce. When a person is saved, they are born again into God's family. God becomes their Father, and Jesus becomes their big brother. They are part of the family of God. And that new believer begins craving milk like a child. They start hungering after God's Word. They begin learning to be more like Jesus. As they mature, they start seeing the world as God sees it. Their heart is moved by what moves the Father's heart, they begin living on mission, they start sharing the gospel with lost friends, they begin investing their lives in others, and they start serving God with their spiritual gifts. Why? Because God commands them to bear spiritual fruit. God commands them to multiply. They have a desire to please God and fulfil the purpose for which they were saved.

This is the normal Christian life. Just like it's normal for children to grow, mature, take a spouse, and start a family. The normal Christian is one who is born again, grows up in a family of believers, spiritually matures, and moves out to invest their life in others. The normal Christian is born to reproduce.

But that's not what we see in most churches today. In most churches we find people who are born into the family but never learn to feed themselves. They are born into the family but never really enjoy deep fellowship with other believers. They are born into the family but never mature. They are born into the family but never move forward to live for God and never know the joy of multiplying their lives. And we see leaders who have lost this vision of multiplication and see their purpose as solely to serve the congregation, not build a movement. From our eyes that's normal, but from heaven's eyes, something is terribly wrong. And this is precisely why we need disciple-making leaders. The disciple-making leader's responsibility is to lead their people and church to multiply, just as Jesus commanded.

THE OWNER, THE WORKER, AND THE FIG TREE

What does God think of a church that never multiplies? Jesus told a parable late in his ministry that tells us what God thinks and what we can do about it. For almost three years Jesus had invested in a few men who would change the world. These men had everything and set out on an adventure to follow Jesus. During this time, he trained them how to walk as he walked, act as he acted, and do as he did. He trained these men to multiply their lives into others, and by the time Jesus told this parable, the movement was already in motion. What Jesus started could not be stopped. But this kind of movement doesn't come without a cost, which is why Jesus spoke often about suffering, self-denial, and sacrifice.

JESUS SPOKE OFTEN ABOUT SUFFERING, SELF-DENIAL, AND SACRIFICE.

And in this context, Jesus told this parable.

> A man had a fig tree planted in his vineyard, and he came seeking fruit on it and found none. And he said to the vinedresser, "Look, for three years now I have come seeking fruit on this fig tree, and I find none. Cut it down. Why should it use up the ground?" And he answered him, "Sir, let it alone this year also, until I dig around it and put on manure. Then if it should bear fruit next year, well and good; but if not, you can cut it down." (Luke 13:6–9, ESV)

This parable is short, to the point, and without a lot of moving parts. There's an owner, a worker, and a barren fig tree. What do these characters represent? Most agree the owner is God. He is the one who owns everything and to whom we must give an account. Most scholars agree the worker represents Jesus. He is the one tending to his people and, by his Spirit, causing the growth.

But what does the barren fig tree represent? Some argue the tree is unrepentant and barren Israel at the time of Christ. They had the prophets and the Scriptures, they had been told of the coming Messiah, yet they did not embrace Jesus. Some say the tree represents unbelievers who have an opportunity to come to Christ but don't bear the fruit of repentance. But what if there is another interpretation? What if this tree represents a church that is barren and doesn't produce disciples? What if this tree represents leaders who continue to ignore Jesus' mandate to make disciples and multiply a movement? What if this story is a warning to you and to me?

Here's the point of the parable: success in Jesus' eyes is all about multiplication. Jesus didn't tell us how large this tree was or how healthy it appeared. This tree could have been the tallest tree in the vineyard. It could have provided shade for the workers and shelter for birds in its branches. This tree could have appeared successful, but it had one problem. It didn't produce any fruit; it failed to multiply. In many ways, this parable is a gut check for all of us that calls for an honest assessment of our lives, our priorities, our leadership, and our churches.

Jesus expects every follower to bear fruit and make disciples. On the night Jesus was betrayed and arrested, he told his disciples, "You did not choose me, but I chose you and appointed you so that you might go and bear fruit—fruit that will last" (John 15:16, NIV). Fruitfulness and multiplication are clearly linked. Fruit-bearing and multiplication are all terms that describe making disciples. This is the fundamental command of Jesus, the "divine imperative" found in the Great Commission. Also, Jesus' final command to his disciples was to make disciples:

> All authority in heaven and on earth has been given to me. Go therefore and make disciples of all nations, baptizing them in the name of the Father and of the Son and of the Holy Spirit, teaching them to observe all I have commanded you. And behold, I am with you always, to the end of the age. (Matt. 28:18–20, ESV)

As I stated before, this command isn't just for pastors and missionaries. This command is for every Christ follower. Jesus expects every follower to bear fruit.

The fig tree in this story had every reason to bear fruit. It was inside a vineyard, had the best soil and water, and even had a caretaker to tend to it. But even still, it did not produce fruit. For three years it had been barren. Many Christians are like that. They have the Scriptures. They go to a great church. They have all the resources and training available to them, but they are fruitless. They don't invest in others, don't share their faith, and don't live on mission. Many churches are also like that. They have impressive facilities and offer great worship services and kids programming, but they never multiply. They are barren.

A few years ago, Liz and I were in Colorado Springs speaking at a conference, and we went to see the gravesite of Dawson Trotman, who had founded the Navigator ministry that discipled hundreds of thousands of men and women after World War II and continues to this day.

Strangely, he died in a freak waterskiing accident in New York in the prime of his ministry. In a now-famous speech he gave, called "Born to Reproduce," he described how the organization evaluated young missionaries before they left for their overseas assignments.

He would ask, "How many persons do you know by name today who were won to Christ by you and are living for him?" The majority had no answer. Many said they had encouraged many people to go to church; others said they had persuaded some to go forward when the invitation was given. Dawson would press further, "Are they living for Christ now?" Their eyes often dropped. Then he'd say, "How do you expect that by crossing an ocean and speaking in a foreign language with people who are suspicious of you, whose way of life is unfamiliar, you will be able to do there what you have not yet done here?" I have read that part of Dawson's speech many times, and every time, I am convicted. God expects each of us to bear fruit that will last.

Robert Coleman, who wrote one of the greatest books on disciple making in recent times, said, "A barren Christian is a contradiction. A tree is known by its fruit. . . . [Fruitlessness] was the thing lacking in the lives of the Sadducees and Pharisees that made them so wretched in his sight."[46] Jesus did not die on the cross, establish his church, and give us the Holy Spirit so we would just attend church. He did it so we would bear fruit. This is our main purpose in life. We are here to share the gospel, invest our lives, make disciples, and fuel the movement until he comes! This is the fruitful life that Jesus calls each of us to live.

And for pastors and ministry leaders, this is the life we are to exemplify, calling others to follow us in it. This is why we so desperately need disciple-making pastors. Because only disciple-making pastors live that investment, and only disciple-making pastors raise up leaders and churches to take the call of Jesus seriously to multiply. Without disciple-making pastors, churches will become like that fruitless fig tree.

There are serious consequences for failing to multiply. A barren church is a disobedient church, and barrenness has its consequences. In this case, the tree was about to be cut down. The owner's words were harsh but true. "It's been three years. Cut it down. It's wasting the soil on which it's planted." This command to bear fruit is so important that failing to do so brings grave consequences. Similar warnings are all throughout the Bible. For example, Jesus said, "Every good tree produces good fruit, . . . [and] every tree that doesn't produce good fruit is cut down and thrown into the fire" (Matt. 7:17, 19). Such a tree is worthless and only good for kindling. Again, in Mark 11:12–14, as Jesus traveled into Jerusalem, he came across a fig tree that was barren, and he cursed the tree because it didn't bear fruit. Jesus said, "He cuts off every branch in me that bears no fruit. . . . If you do not remain in me, you are like a branch that is thrown away and withers; such branches are picked up, thrown into the fire and burned" (John 15:2, 6, NIV). You get the picture? Failure to bear fruit, failure to invest, and failure to multiply is serious business. I'm not saying that Christians who never multiply their lives lose their salvation, but the Bible repeatedly warns us that failing to do what Jesus commanded is a serious offense.

If that's the case, then why don't most Christians multiply? The excuses are broad and wide. Some claim they are too busy. Others say they wouldn't know what to do. Still others excuse themselves because they have never seen an invested life before. Much of it comes down to what Jesus pointed out in John 15:7–8: "If you remain in me and my words remain in you, ask whatever you want and it will be done for you. My Father is glorified by this: that you produce much fruit and prove to be my disciples." When I spend time with Jesus, when I make my home with him, when I pray, "Jesus, show me your heart. I want what you want. I want to be the person you want me to be," he puts the desire in my heart to share the gospel. He brings people to mind I can disciple. He prompts me by his Spirit. But if I'm not walking closely with Jesus, then my heart drifts and the excuses come. Distractions creep in. The call to make disciples becomes a burden, an obligation, a duty rather than an act of love.

Jesus said that true disciples will produce fruit. Fruitfulness is the test of discipleship. And only this kind of fruitfulness can change our world. A multiplying church is a catalyst for change that ultimately brings transformation to communities, cities, and countries.

FRUITFULNESS IS THE TEST OF DISCIPLESHIP.

Fruit in a barren place. Montreal is one of the spiritually darkest cities in North America. Less than half a percent of the population has been reached by the gospel. Much of its resistance stems from the historic abuses of the government-controlled Catholic Church. This oppressive religious control combined with a relentless dynastic monarchy that fueled the horrific, blood-stained French Revolution of the late 1700s. The remaining vestiges of religion were finally cast off 160 years later in the Quiet Revolution. Later, following the elections of 1960, Quebec swiftly embraced political changes, which produced a more secularized welfare state. These changes included the removal of the Catholic Church from public healthcare and education. Along with the removal of religious influence came the removal of people from the churches. In one day, the people of Montreal left the Catholic Church, never to return. Many of the churches still today remain empty shells of what they once were.

This social transition is depicted vividly in Montreal's most celebrated piece of art, *The Illuminated Crowd.* This large statue, by artist Raymond Mason, sits at the entrance gate to McGill University along one of Montreal's busiest streets. The sculpture reflects the fragility of humanity and the longing for hope. The statue consists of sixty-five individuals of all ages and ethnicities closely compacted together. The back of the crowd portrays various forms of perversity and violence, disorder, shame, and despair. Toward the middle of the crowd, people's expressions change, embracing one another in peace. At the front of the crowd a man stands tall, pointing to what lies ahead as people look forward in hope. In many ways this statue reflects the mindset of the Quebecois people. The Quiet Revolution was a rejection of religion with its past abuses and violence and a turning toward the brighter hope of secularism. No wonder, then, most of the curse words in the French language find some root in the Catholic Church. The resentment still remains.

It was in this place that Claude Houde planted a church in the village of Longueuil, on the southern shore of Montreal. Claude had been discipled by David Wilkerson, the famous American evangelist and author of the book *The Cross and the Switchblade*. The church was called *Nouvelle Vie* ("New Life"). It was a small congregation in a small building, but God was able to use this man to do the impossible. And this miracle began in a snowstorm.

They call it the Great Ice Storm of 1998. Brutal winds and freezing temperatures pressed down hard on parts of Canada, lower Quebec, and New England, leaving behind devastated infrastructure and downed power lines. The damage was so severe that more Canadian military forces were deployed in the recovery effort than at any time since the Korean War. Miraculously, Pastor Claude was able to retain power and, through the prompting of an older woman in their village, opened the doors of the church to those suffering in the cold. People packed into their small building. Blankets and hot drinks were tangible expressions of comfort. So many were cared for during the crisis that the mayor of Longueuil recognized the church and offered a check for one million dollars.

Suddenly and inexplicably, the church began growing, and many people came to Christ. A Bible college was started to train men and women to take the gospel to the people of Quebec. People sensed that God was doing something new and exciting. At this time, Claude began discipling a young man named David Pothier. David was full of passion and a dynamic communicator. As Claude invested in David, he could see unbridled potential. Soon he asked David to move into leadership, speaking to young adults who came to the church. It wasn't long before many came to Christ under his preaching. And as the church grew, so did David's popularity.

God moved in unprecedented ways. After a prayer meeting, Claude told David, "You are going to be our first church planter." These words only affirmed what was already stirring deep in David's heart. He wanted to plant a church that would reach people for Christ and ignite a disciple-making movement. But he didn't want to plant in Montreal.

David had grown up outside the metropolitan bustle of the big city in a small, rural community called *Trois-Rivières* ("Three Rivers"). He had no interest in the urban center of Montreal with its towering skyscrapers and loud subways. However, God moved, and David's heart was softened. God gave him a vision of a church that would reach the people who had turned their backs on God a long time ago.

The first pre-launch of the church took place in a bar. Just cleaning the place to prepare for the gathering was dangerous. Used needles on the floor, the smell of alcohol, and even the hanging disco ball were all reminders of what had taken place the night before and the condition of the souls of the city. Like *The Illuminated Crowd*, people were desperate for someone to point them to real hope. To everyone's amazement, two hundred showed up for the first pre-launch service. Three hundred came to the next gathering. Clearly, the small bar was not going to be large enough to hold this type of crowd. Before the official launch date, David told the people, "You know the people who need to be here. Go get them and bring them!" Since the small bar was not able to hold this large a crowd, David moved the official launch of the church to a public high school. That Sunday, more than five hundred people packed into the theater in addition to people standing in the lobby. David turned to a friend and said, "This is only the beginning!" They called the new church *la Chapelle* ("the Chapel").

This was a new church committed to reaching a new generation with the gospel. David's vision was not only to grow a large church but also to begin a church-planting center that would multiply disciple-making churches across Montreal and the larger French-speaking world. But how would they do that? The small church rented office space above a gym and started dreaming. It became clear that *la Chapelle* would have to intentionally raise up disciple-making leaders if they were to multiply. David took ten men to invest in and develop personally as leaders, walking them through the discipleship pathway. Other staff members did the same. As these men grew in their faith, they rose up the leadership pipeline. Many went off to plant churches and raise up leaders as well. Today the church continues to grow and make progress on their vision to plant one hundred churches in the next thirty years. David was driven by the command of Jesus to make disciples and build a movement. And if you ask him today, he will tell you there is no greater joy than multiplying your life.

As our country grows increasingly dark both morally and spiritually, the remedies are disciple-making churches led by disciple-making leaders. Now more than ever, we need disciple-making leaders like David and Henri. We need leaders who genuinely walk with Jesus, preach the gospel, sacrifice to make multiplication a reality, and invest in other leaders to reproduce in kind. This is the need of the hour. This is the need of our nation. And this is what will cause all of heaven to erupt in joyful praise to God.

God's greatest rewards are for those who multiply. Looking back again at Jesus' parable of the fig tree, the story stops short of what you would expect. We are never told if the tree ever bore fruit. We aren't even told the owner's response to the worker's request. It ends with a cliffhanger. Jesus likely did this because in many ways our lives are like this too. For example, the end of your story is yet to be written. Will you give your life to following Jesus and making disciples? Will you multiply your life? Some will and some will not. You may be like David in Montreal or Henri in Burkina Faso—you may have lasting fruit to show for your single life, lasting fruit to give to Christ when you enter heaven. Or you may have little to show. But never forget: God rewards the fruitful life.

In many ways, God still rewards us in this life. A deep love and satisfaction come with knowing that God is using you. What keeps me in ministry is not the big events our church does each year or the leadership challenges or the caring for hurting people. What keeps me in ministry is the incredible satisfaction of knowing I have invested in a few, and they are doing the same, and the kingdom is growing as a result. I have invested my life into several men who are making a difference, and that brings me great joy. The apostle John writes: "I have no greater joy than to hear that my children are walking in the truth" (3 John 1:4, ESV). He wasn't talking about his biological children because he never married. Instead, he was talking about the people he had invested in who walked with God. That is a joy that cannot be fully measured. The greatest joys in life come when you multiply. The greatest love is when you invest in another person to help them grow. Just like being a parent, the joys of being a spiritual parent are innumerable.

But there is a reward and a joy from multiplication that we will experience in heaven. To those he invests his life in, Paul says, "For what is our hope, our joy, or the crown in which we will glory in the presence of our Lord Jesus when he comes? Is it not you?" (1 Thess. 2:19, NIV). The day of my youngest daughter's wedding was one of the happiest days of my life. The venue was a lush botanical garden that sat like an oasis on the barren Texas prairie. Beautiful fountains and reflective pools were surrounded by dark green hedges and blossoms of color. The ceremony took place on a manicured lawn, under an arch of white hydrangeas, roses, and peonies. The reception was under a massive white tent that stretched out in a large rectangle with two large peaks. We were surrounded by the people we loved. Many old friends who had known our daughter from birth were there, celebrating alongside new friends she had just met in college. The joy was palpable.

Sometime during the evening, my new son-in-law came up beside me and said with a smile, "Hey, I thought you might like to meet some of your grandchildren." Behind him stood three young men he had discipled while in college, who were, in turn, about to launch new disciple-making groups in the fall. I encouraged them for a bit and thanked them for their willingness to follow Jesus and join his movement. As they turned back to their table, I couldn't help but reflect on the moment. Here I was amid a wedding celebration, meeting young men who had been impacted by my influence, and I hadn't even known it.

This is what heaven is going to be like. It will be like a huge wedding celebration (Matt. 22:1–14). Jesus, the groom, and his bride, the church, will join together in a cosmic celebration of love and grace to the Father's approval and delight. And in that moment of celebration, if you have multiplied your life in others and lived for the movement, you will meet people you never met on earth but who are there because of your influence. You will meet your spiritual grandchildren and great-great-grandchildren. You will hear how your one life touched another, who touched another, who touched another, who touched them. This is one of the things that will make heaven so exciting. All because you didn't waste your life, didn't make excuses, didn't allow distractions to rob you of your eternal purpose, and you lived a fruitful life.

THE MOVEMENTS OF TOMORROW

Throughout this book I have given you glimpses into movements that God fanned into flame throughout church history and around the world. The apostle Paul, Ignatius, St. Patrick, Martin Luther, John Wesley, Dietrich Bonhoeffer, Bill Bright, Dion Robert, Haik Mehr—each of these men lived in their own times and circumstances. Each of these men chose to be disciple-making leaders and kingdom builders. They faced opposition with great faith and discouragement with eternal hope. They made disciples in their lifetime, and then their time was over.

Now it is your time. This is your moment. How will you live it?

The great movements of the past were led by disciple-making leaders. They transformed their cultures, pushed back the darkness, and multiplied churches until they became an unstoppable movement. And the great movements of tomorrow will also be led by disciple-making leaders. The movements of God yet to be realized will come at the hands of disciple-making leaders who invest their lives and multiply the church.

Charles Thomas Studd, the British cricket player and missionary to China, wrote a profound poem titled "Only One Life." The refrain repeats, "Only one life, 'twill soon be past. Only what's done for Christ will last." You only have one life. It is fleeting and will be over sooner than you think. How will you live your life? What will you have to show

Jesus when you stand before him? Are you bearing lasting fruit? Are you multiplying your life and the ministry you lead?

The life well lived is the invested life. It is not the life of celebrity, not the life of the superstar, and not the life of comfort. It is the life which, over the course of days, weeks, months, and years, consistently invests in others and teaches them to do the same. This is the life that will ignite movements and shape the eternal destinies of countless men and women. This is the work of Jesus. This is what matters most.

THE LIFE WELL LIVED IS THE INVESTED LIFE.

And it matters most, not because your or my contribution is that great, but because we serve a great God who has promised that when we multiply our lives for his movement, he will use us in greater ways than we can possibly imagine. The great spiritual movements of the past are just that . . . they are in the past. But great movements are still ahead. God's greatest works are yet to be seen.

And whom will he work through to bring about those great movements? On whom will his providential eye rest when he looks for someone to use? Just maybe he will use you. Maybe he will find you walking with him deeply, making disciples, building his movement, and producing disciple-making leaders. I pray that this will be true both in your life and in mine.

GROUP DISCUSSION QUESTIONS

1. Why do many pastors and ministry leaders lack a multiplication mindset?
2. What in this chapter stands out to you the most about Jesus' view of multiplication?
3. In what areas of your ministry do you need to multiply and raise up new leaders?
4. Based on what you've learned in this book, what next steps do you need to take to develop disciple-making leaders?
5. What challenges will you face?
6. What will motivate you to overcome these challenges and produce disciple-making leaders in every level of leadership?

CONCLUSION

If "everything rises or falls on leadership," then understanding why Jesus spent so much time investing, training, and developing his leaders to multiply is easy. He knew the future of the movement depended on the leaders he developed. He knew his kingdom wouldn't be built on the shoulders of superstars who gained the attention of the culture; instead, the kingdom would be built by disciple-making leaders who multiplied their lives into the lives of others and sacrificed their lives for his great cause.

Jesus knew this. And it's still true today.

GOD'S MOVEMENTS IN THE FUTURE ARE ROOTED IN THE PAST.

God's movements in the future are rooted in the past. The leaders of the future will have the same DNA of those early church leaders. They will be men and women who know how to develop disciple-making leaders at every level of their ministry.

In the first chapter I defined a disciple-making leader as one who leads out of the overflow of their walk with Christ and intentionally invests in others to produce genuine disciples and ministry leaders who will multiply the movement. These were the kinds of leaders Jesus produced. He invested his life in men who would walk with him intimately, invest their lives personally, and raise up leaders intentionally. Those leaders eventually changed the world.

You might ask, "So how do I put this into practice in my own ministry area?" Let me offer you a few practical steps of application.

First, solidify your disciple-making pathway. This pathway will provide you the road map to help people grow spiritually in your church or ministry. And even if your whole church doesn't have (or embrace) such a pathway, you can still implement it in certain departments. Make it clear, keep it simple, and communicate it often. Align your programming to the pathway so you know how to develop people at every stage in the process. This may take time, but it is worth it. You can't produce disciple-making leaders until you have a clear pathway to produce disciple makers.

Second, clarify your leadership pipeline. Obviously, the size of your church or ministry will determine the number of levels of leadership you utilize. Some large, multi-site churches may have more than five levels, and smaller ones may have less. However, begin with the five leadership levels mentioned in this book. After you identify these levels, build out your pipeline. Identify leaders at every level, and note the areas where you have gaps that need filling. Draw out a diagram that shows every position of leadership in your area and every person in your ministry and where they fit in your pipeline. Clarify the skills you need at each level. Solidify your process for recruiting, assessing, preparing, and supporting those leaders. Begin looking for key leaders who can move up in your organization.

After you have the pathway and pipeline intact, you're ready for the third step. Begin training leaders at every level of leadership with the methods mentioned in this book. Think of the pathway and pipeline like rails for a train. After they are laid, you can use them to identify and develop leaders who will multiply the ministry. The back half of this book is broken down into chapters on how to develop leaders at every level of your ministry organization. Start using this material to invest in them.

You might ask, "Where should I begin?" Start at the top. If you are an Organization Leader, start reading this book with your Department Leaders and implementing these principles. Then coach how to incorporate these principles into Leaders of Leaders, Team Leaders, and ultimately, Self-Leaders. If you are a Department Leader, then share these principles with your team and develop the leaders under you. Remember, only elevate a person into leadership to the degree that they have progressed down the pathway.

Last, study the life of Jesus along your journey. Get a *Harmony of the Gospels*. Study what Jesus did in year one, year two, and year three. Emulate his methods as your pattern for ministry. Learn from his example. At the back of this book are a few resources on the life of Christ, namely the key scriptures in each phase of his ministry training. I hope these will assist your study. My friend likes to say, "Jesus is a deep well." This is so true. The more you follow the Master and imitate his life, the more you will find the strength and resolve to invest in leaders like he did.

In the opening pages I said, "The future movements of tomorrow rely on disciple-making leaders." I truly believe that. As I look over the past twenty-five years of ministry, I can honestly say my greatest joy has come in investing my life in people. And when I see them investing in others, nothing gets get better than that. This is how the movement grows and how the kingdom advances: one life at a time.

We have seen movements of God in the past. This is for sure. But great movements are still ahead. Great things are yet to come. Greater things are still to be done. And these great future movements will be done by disciple-making leaders who walk with God, invest their lives, and produce leaders after them who change the world. May the unbroken chain of your investment continue to multiply until Jesus comes. And if by chance we are here when he comes back, may he find us faithful, making disciples and building his movement.

APPENDIX A

THE OPTIMAL DISCIPLE-MAKING STRUCTURE

Environments shape experience. A plant requires a great environment to grow and be healthy. A place with plenty of sunlight, where it can be watered regularly. However, if you put that plant in a closet and forget about it, it will die quickly. The same is true when it comes to spiritual growth. Those who grow spiritually find environments that foster healthy growth. And I strongly believe three key environments best facilitate this kind of growth. Usually, I refer to this as the 3C model for church health and growth.

CELEBRATION

The first environment requires "celebrations." These are large group gatherings where the Bible is taught and believers are encouraged through corporate prayer and worship.

We see large gatherings like this in the book of Acts. Shortly after the birth of the church, new believers gathered for teaching and encouragement daily (Acts 2:46). In this environment they devoted themselves to the apostles' teaching, to prayer, to breaking bread together, and to biblical community (Acts 2:42). The apostles' message was authenticated by miraculous signs and wonders, and daily the Lord added new believers to their number (Acts 2:43, 47).

This celebration is important for corporate expressions of worship, the declaration of the gospel, and the teaching of God's Word. Most churches offer a gathering like this on Sunday mornings. While some gatherings are larger than others, the collective nature sets it apart from other environments. Over the years, I've had the privilege of gathering with believers in cathedrals of Rome, cinder-block buildings in Africa, remote churches in the hills of Cuba, and a converted bar in Montreal, Canada. I've seen firsthand how every church has its own unique expression and contributes to the beautiful mosaic of God's kingdom. And in each place, I have felt the warmth of community and the presence of God's Spirit.

We experience something together corporately that is unique from what we experience alone or even in a small group. As mentioned earlier, after John Wesley preached to the masses in outdoor venues, he invited all to attend corporate gatherings he called "societies." There the Bible was preached, songs were sung that related to biblical truth, and corporate forms of worship, such as prayer and giving, were encouraged. This environment roots the new believer in the notion that they are part of a larger family and community of faith.

CONGREGATION

The second environment requires "congregations." Here believers are encouraged to meet in smaller groups ranging from ten to thirty people. In this environment a big church becomes small, and the roots of relationships grow deep.

After the early church gathered in large public meetings for corporate worship, they "broke bread from house to house. They ate their food with joyful and sincere hearts, praising God and enjoying the favor of all the people" (Acts 2:46–47). Most homes in that day could not accommodate large crowds and were likely limited to ten to twenty people. In these homes, the believers encouraged each other, ate together, expressed their sincere faith, praised God, and shared their belongings with each other. If anyone had a need, the group met the need. If anyone was in trouble, the community of believers worked together to resolve the matter.

Wesley employed this environment as well. Those who attended societies were also encouraged to attend "class" meetings, groups comprised of twelve to fifteen men and women, all there for the purpose of caring for one another and encouraging spiritual growth. These home meetings created a safe place to know and be known, care and be cared for, love and be loved, serve and be served. We are created for community, and in a world where relationships are fragmented and people are often sequestered, this environment satisfies the needs of the soul.

When Pastor Dion Robert began his church in Abidjan, he organized it around home groups. These groups welcomed neighbors who asked spiritual questions, and the groups fervently shared the gospel with them. These groups also nurtured new believers and spoke on their behalf at their baptisms. They became a family to many who had no family. When a church member left the city to settle in another city or country, they were encouraged not to join a church but rather to start a group in their home. Through this method, the church multiplied to nations all over the world.

Thus, people need a corporate celebration experience, but they also need a smaller congregation to care for them and nurture their souls.

CELL

The third environment requires "cells." These are smaller, gender-specific groups, ranging from three to five people. Here men gather with men and women with women for the purpose of equipping them for leadership development and spiritual multiplication.

When the early church faced a conflict that threatened to split it along racial lines, seven men rose to leadership to quiet the people and heal the rift. These men had been cultivated and were readily recognized as leaders by the congregation. Where did they come from? While we are not told, my guess is they had been trained and cultivated by the apostles, who had, in turn, been trained and cultivated by Jesus. This was the counterintuitive genius of Jesus. If you were going to start a movement to reach the ends of the earth, you might think you need to spend time with large groups of people and mobilize the masses. Jesus, however, did the opposite. He went smaller, not larger. He selected a few men and devoted most of his time to training and equipping them to multiply themselves into others.

This strategy was replicated throughout church history. Paul encouraged young Timothy to take what he had learned from him and entrust it to faithful men who would teach others (2 Tim. 2:2). Patrick trained new believers in Ireland to be church planters and brought them along with him to new villages. Luther drew his students around his dinner table and invested in them. Wesley created a third environment called "bands," where he trained men with men and women with women for the purpose of expanding the movement and multiplying churches. Bill Bright used this same strategy on university campuses to create an international movement. And churches today follow this same strategy to create movements of multiplication.

I am so thankful for the men in my life who took time to come alongside me and show me how to walk with God in a genuine way. These men taught me how to journal and pray. They showed me how to share my faith and stand against temptation. I saw these things lived out in their lives, and they inspired me to invest my life in others. For the past thirty years, I've been investing my life in men, and I've seen lives changed forever. There is something about this environment that fosters incredible spiritual growth and produces multiplying disciple makers.

While every environment is important in the disciple-making process, the use of cells for transformation cannot be overstated. Greg Ogden, who has written extensively on disciple making, calls these cells "hot houses of the Holy Spirit." Just as a "greenhouse" provides the optimal environment for growth, the small cell provides the optimal environment for spiritual growth. In these small groups, believers find prayer, encouragement, accountability, and training, all the things necessary to be transformed into the image of Jesus.

PUTTING THE ENVIRONMENTS TOGETHER

Disciple-making leaders must utilize disciple-making environments to produce spiritual growth and rapid multiplication. Each of these environments is necessary to have a healthy, multiplying, disciple-making church. Now, you might think, *I don't really need to have each of these elements in my church. One or two will suffice.* Or, *I can barely get my people to attend one of these a week, much less three!* But let's take a deeper look at why all three are important.

First, each environment is intentional. Each environment exists to produce something unique and necessary in the life of a believer. Whereas the celebration environment allows new believers to grow and exposes them to God's Word, the congregation environment roots the believer in truth and community, and the cell environment provides the needed training and accountability for leadership development. Each of these environments provides something special the others cannot. And certainly, one environment can't provide all that is needed on its own.

Let's look at this from another perspective. Suppose you want to take up running because you know it will be good for your health. So you sign up for a 5K race in your community. On the day of the race, you are with the large crowd of people, and you can feel the excitement in the air. You pin your number to your shirt and stretch a little before the race. When the gun goes off, you are part of a stream of runners flowing through the streets. You feel part of something bigger than yourself. You see all kinds of people around you, older and younger, large and skinny, but you are all caught up in this moment together, running the race and doing your best.

This inspires you to join a local running club. And there you meet people who share your passion for running. You grow close to these people on long runs, sharing not only tips for better running but also your personal lives as well. These are your people. Your tribe. Your community. When someone misses a run, the others call to check up on them. When one is sick, the others take a meal. The running group becomes a real family.

But as you improve, suppose the instructor of the running club sees potential in you. He invites you to a special training every Saturday for the next three months to up your game and prepare you to lead a running club of your own. The training is intense. You are pushed beyond what you thought possible. You learn techniques on managing people, coaching runners, treating chronic running injuries, and responding to emergency situations. After three months you are assigned to lead a running club of your own.

Each of these environments gave you something special that you needed to grow as a runner and a leader. The big race inspired you and made you feel part of something larger than yourself. The club gave you community and pushed you to keep running and growing. The training stretched you and gave you the tools to become a leader and help others enjoy running. Each environment played a special role. The same is true in your spiritual life. Each environment is intentionally designed to grow you in a special facet of your walk with Jesus and prepare you for the next step on your journey.

Second, each environment is sequential. That is, one naturally leads to the next, which leads to the next. Skipping steps seldom produces the results you want. Back to the running illustration. If you had jumped from the 5K to the intense leader training, you would have probably quit after the first day. The community aspect was a vital ingredient in your development as a runner. The same is true spiritually.

The natural sequence of spiritual growth usually begins with an invitation to a church gathering where the gospel is preached. Once inspired by the large group, a person is usually open to trying a smaller group of people who share the same stage of life or similar interests. For example, most of the congregational type groups in our church are based on stages of life, namely single, young married, parents, empty nesters, and senior adults. Others may be formed around interests like a common neighborhood, school district, or activity. As a believer grows in these environments, they become open to a more challenging cell group where they can develop the skills they need to invest in others and multiply. The sequential nature of these groups is important because each environment represents the next step along their spiritual pathway.

Third, each of these environments is essential. Some have proposed that three is not necessary because a church can multiply disciples with only one or two of them. But I have never seen this done effectively. Of course, examples are throughout church history of times when small house churches spread rapidly without large group gatherings. These usually took place under hostile conditions where the church was openly persecuted. There were also times when only large group gatherings were offered to church members, and only a selected group were sent for training, mostly to seminaries or monasteries. God's church has always found a way to adapt and grow, even in the worst of circumstances.

But overall, the healthiest churches provide these three healthy environments. In each environment, people find an essential element of their spiritual growth. The large group provides inspiration, the small group provides community and encouragement, and the cell provides accountability and training. All three are vital to producing multiplying disciples. They are like a three-legged stool: take one out and its purpose fails. In many ways, a believer who is deprived of one of these three environments lacks the full training necessary to fulfill their God-given purpose.

Q&A ABOUT A DISCIPLE-MAKING STRUCTURE

Q: Isn't it enough just to offer a corporate worship gathering and small groups?

A: Some have argued that a church only needs a centralized celebration environment (corporate worship) and a decentralized congregation environment (small groups). However, in my experience, as the home groups meet, those who desire more training usually find another environment in which to be trained. A guy in the group will meet another guy at a coffee shop, or two ladies will meet outside the home group. Then a mature believer can begin investing personally in an eager believer and help them develop skills they need to grow and multiply, which is an example of a cell being formed. Some churches utilize larger leadership trainings on campus to help people develop skills. Again, this creates a third environment for leadership development. So these three environments are necessary for a healthy, multiplying church.

Q: How do you get people to attend three environments a week?

A: This is a common question. Most agree the corporate worship experience is what people attend regularly. A smaller group environment may be a stretch, but doable, depending on where and when the group meets and if childcare is available. But many churches think the cell environment won't work because people are too busy. Remember, the cell is where leaders are trained and multiplication happens. Also, while the celebration and congregation environments are ongoing, the cell is only for a specific period. In our church, a cell lasts about nine months, taking breaks for holidays. If you give people something they want, they will make time for it. For example, I have friends who go to the gym at 4:00 a.m. every day. Why do they do that? Obviously, because it's important to them, and they can see the results. People will do the same thing with their spiritual growth. If they want to grow and can see results, they will do whatever it takes, even if that means adding another meeting to their schedule. If the cell is too similar to a small group, or redundant, they will drop out.

Q: Aren't home groups and cell groups the same?

A: Not necessarily. Small groups are designed to build up the believers through Bible study, care, and service opportunities. They are open groups, meaning they invite people to join at any time, and they are continuous, without any specified ending date. Because they are open and continuous, the accountability in these groups is very low. Just show up and participate. However, cell groups are very different. These groups are much smaller, with three to five members, and are designed to equip leaders to multiply and prepare them for leadership. Consequently, these groups are open only to those who agree to participate. The accountability is high, and the content is focused on core competencies needed to multiply and lead. Since the goal here is multiplication and leadership, these groups have a definitive ending date.

APPENDIX B

KEY EVENTS IN THE LIFE OF JESUS

The central figure in Christianity is Jesus. And the majority of what we know about Jesus comes from the Gospels, the first four books in the New Testament: Matthew, Mark, Luke, and John. While each of these books is rooted in history and based on eyewitness accounts, each provides a different perspective of the life of Jesus. Matthew was written primarily to a Jewish audience, and the material is often organized thematically. Mark was written to a Greek audience and focuses on the actions of Jesus. Luke was written to a Roman audience and is the most chronological. And John was written much later and fills in the gaps in Jesus' timeline. It also reveals a more in-depth account of Jesus' final hours.

While the life of Jesus can be understood from reading each of these accounts separately, when you read all four Gospels in chronological order, Jesus' model becomes shockingly clear. According to Robert Thomas and Stanley Gundry, "A harmony of the gospels provides an important means for studying the four gospels at one time. Though it could never completely replace the four gospels studied individually, it is an indispensable tool for gaining a well-rounded overview of Jesus' life in all its facets."[47]

30 KEY EVENTS IN THE LIFE OF JESUS

	MT	MK	L	J
1. Birth	1:18–25		2:1–7	
2. Teaching in temple			2:41–50	
3. Baptism	3:13–17	1:9–11	3:21–22	
4. Temptation	4:1–11	1:12–13	4:1–3	
5. First followers				1:35–51
6. Miracle at Cana				2:1–11
7. Nicodemus				3:1–21
8. Samaritan woman				4:5–38
9. Rejection in Nazareth			4:16–30	
10. Call of the four	4:18–22	1:16–20		
11. Heals Peter's mother-in-law	8:14–17	1:29–34	4:38 –41	
12. Second call			5:1–11	
13. Call of Matthew	9:9	2:13 –14	5:27–28	
14. Appointment of apostles		3:1–19		
15. Tour with the Twelve			8:1–3	
16. Healing of demoniac	8:28–34	5:1–20	8:26–39	
17. Sending of the Twelve	10:1–42	6:7–13	9:1–6	
18. Feeding five thousand	14:15–21	6:35–44	9:12–17	6:4–13
19. Caesarea Philippi	16:13–20	8:27–30	9:18–20	
20. Transfiguration	17:1–8	9:2–13	9:28–36	
21. Feast of Tabernacles				7:10–8:59
22. Sending the Seventy-Two			10:1–16	
23. Feast of Dedication				10:22–39
24. Raising of Lazarus				11:17–44
25. Triumphal entry	21:1–17	11:1–11	19:29–44	12:12–19
26. Upper room	26:17–29	14:12–25	22:7–23	13–17
27. Crucifixion	27:27–56	15:16–41	23:26–49	19:16–30
28. Resurrection	28:1–10	16:1–8	24:1–12	20:1–10
29. Great Commission	28:16–20			
30. Ascension			24:50–53	

EXPLORE PHASE

The arrival of Jesus didn't happen in isolation. The whole nation had been waiting for the Messiah. Ever since the fall of man (Gen. 3), sin had tainted and twisted the world God created. But even in the garden of Eden, God spoke of when one would come and crush Satan's head and suffer unto death. This prophecy echoed throughout the centuries. A Messiah would come deliver his people. He would suffer for the sins of the world and set his people free.

John the Baptist marked a new era in redemptive history. While other prophets spoke of a day when the Messiah would come, John's message was "Here he is! The Lamb of God who takes away the sin of the world has come!" In many ways, he was the last Old Testament prophet and a new day had dawned. The Son of God had come!

During the eighteen months of his ministry, Jesus engaged spiritual explorers of all kinds, confronting them with his claim of messiahship. He confronted the poor and wealthy, the outcast and elite, and the skeptic and the believer, answering their spiritual questions and revealing the truth that he was the promised one about whom the law and prophets had testified.

Phase: Explore
Phrase: "Come and see."
Verse: John 1:39
Time: Eighteen months

TEN KEY EVENTS DURING THE EXPLORE PHASE OF JESUS' MINISTRY

1. *Jesus' baptism (Matt. 3:13–17; Mark 1.9–11; Luke 3.21–23)*
2. *Jesus' temptation (Matt. 4:1–11; Mark 1:12–13; Luke 4:1–13)*
3. *Jesus called his first followers (John 1:35–51)*
4. *Miracle at Cana (John 2:1–11)*
5. Jesus journeyed to Capernaum for a few days (John 2:12)
6. Jesus cleansed the temple (John 2:13–22)

7. *Jesus met with Nicodemus (John 3:1–21)*
8. *Jesus and the Samaritan woman (John 4:5–42)*
9. Jesus healed a nobleman's son (John 4:46–54)
10. *Jesus rejected in Nazareth (John 4:16–31)*

**Italics indicate the events that are included in the top thirty events of the life of Jesus*

CONNECT PHASE

Following his first eighteen months of ministry, Jesus settled in the larger city of Capernaum and began choosing his leadership team. Up to this point, these men had been following Jesus and fishing for a living. But now Jesus called them to a higher level of commitment, to leave their nets and fish for men.

As these men followed Jesus, they made three key commitments. First was the commitment to Jesus himself. They learned more and more that Jesus was who he claimed to be, the promised Messiah. Second was their commitment to each other. From this time forward, they lived in community. And third was their commitment to join the cause of igniting a worldwide movement.

But before they could lead, they had to learn. So during the next six months, these men shadowed Jesus. They learned from him, listened to his teaching, and participated in his ministry. Jesus did the heavy lifting of ministry as they watched, observed, and grew.

Phase: Connect
Phrase: "Follow me."
Verse: Matthew 4:18–19
Time: Six months

FIVE KEY EVENTS/THEMES DURING THE CONNECT PHASE OF JESUS' MINISTRY

1. Jesus settled in Capernaum (Matt. 4:12–15)
2. *Jesus called the first four disciples (Matt. 4:18–22)*
3. Jesus took disciples on "six fishing trips" (Luke 4–5)
    - Demon-possessed man in synagogue (Luke 4:31–37)
    - *Healed Peter's mother-in-law (Luke 4:38–39)*
    - *Second call (Luke 5:1–11)*
    - Cleansed a leper (Luke 5:12–16)
    - Healed a paralytic (Luke 5:17–26)
    - *Called Matthew (Luke 5:27–28)*
4. Controversies over Sabbath
    - Healed a lame man on the Sabbath (John 5:1–9)
    - Picked grain on the Sabbath (Matt. 12:1–8; Mark 2:23–28; Luke 6:1–5)
    - Healed a withered hand on the Sabbath (Matt. 12:9–14; Mark 3:1–6; Luke 6:6–11)
5. Jesus withdrew to the Sea of Galilee (Matt. 12:15; Mark 3:7–12)

**Italics indicate the events that are included in the top thirty events of the life of Jesus*

GROW PHASE

Two full years had passed since Jesus launched his ministry. The crowds had grown, the conflict with religious leaders had intensified, and now Jesus focused more than ever on developing the next leaders of the movement. After a night of prayer, Jesus designated twelve men as apostles so they might "be with" him (Mark 3:13–14) and learn how to lead. The next six months give a glimpse into Jesus' leadership bootcamp. His purpose was to train these men to lead the movement long after he was gone.

Jesus trained his men in three basic ways. First, he trained them by demonstrating his power over the natural world, the spiritual world, religious leaders, and death itself. Jesus wanted them to know all authority had been given to him. Second, Jesus trained them by teaching. The teaching ministry of Jesus exploded during this phase. Jesus taught through long discourses such as the Sermon on the Mount and short stories such as the parables. In this way Jesus taught the disciples what living in the kingdom of God looks like. Third, Jesus trained his men through modeling. Up to this point these men had "shadowed" Jesus, but now he modeled what to do (Luke 8:1), and then released them to do it on their own (Luke 9:1–6).

Along the way these disciples grew in the character of Jesus. Internally, they learned to think as he thought and see the world as he saw it. But they also grew in the competencies of Jesus. They began grasping how to walk with God, reach their world, and invest in a few. These skills proved critical to multiplying the movement.

Phase: Grow
Phrase: "Be with me."
Verse: Mark 3:13–14
Time: Six months

12 KEY EVENTS DURING THE GROW PHASE OF JESUS' MINISTRY

1. *Appointed apostles (Mark 3:13–19; Luke 6:12–16)*
2. Sermon on the Mount (Matt. 5–7; Luke 6:17–31)
3. Healed centurion's servant (Matt. 8:5–13; Luke 7:1–10)
4. *Toured with the Twelve (Luke 8:1–3)*
5. Taught parables (Matt. 13:1–52; Mark 4:1–34; Luke 8:4–18)
6. *Healed demoniac (Matt. 8:28–34; Mark 5:1–20; Luke 8:26–39)*
7. *Sent the Twelve (Matt. 10:1–42; Mark 6:7–11; Luke 9:1–5)*
8. Death of John the Baptist (Matt. 14:3–12; Mark 6:17–29)
9. *Fed five thousand (Matt. 14:15–21; Mark 6:35–44; Luke 9:12–17; John 6:4–13)*
10. Walked on water (Matt. 14:24–33; Mark 6:47–52; John 6:16–21)

11. Some disciples defected (John 6:60–71)
12. Fed four thousand in Decapolis (Matt. 15:32–38; Mark 8:1–9)

**Italics indicate the events that are included in the top thirty events of the life of Jesus*

MULTIPLY PHASE

Jesus now moved into the final phase of his earthly ministry. What had begun as a conversation with his Father in the small northern village of Nazareth was now headed to a great conflict in the streets of Jerusalem. So Jesus pulled his men away, up to the far northern region, to Caesarea Philippi. Here Jesus asked who his disciples believed him to be, and Peter declared him to be the Christ. Upon that declaration, Jesus said he would build the church. But between them and the birth of the church was the cross, so Jesus turned his heart toward the cross: "If anyone would come after me, let him deny himself and take up his cross daily and follow me" (Luke 9:23, ESV).

With only nine months left on earth, Jesus intensified his efforts to ignite a movement of multiplication. First, he prepared his men to endure hardship. Three times he overtly predicted his death, burial, and resurrection. He taught his men the importance of suffering, sacrifice, and self-denial, without which would be no lasting fruit or spiritual multiplication (John 12:24). Second, Jesus multiplied the Twelve into Seventy-Two, and then sent them out to preach the gospel and exercise authority over the demonic. In doing so, Jesus extended the movement by multiplying to the fourth generation (Jesus, the Twelve, the Seventy-Two, and those who would believe), which filled Jesus with joy (Luke 10:21). Last, Jesus boldly declared his identity and purpose. He said he was the Light of the World, the source of Living Water, the Door, and the Good Shepherd who gives his life for the sheep. He proclaimed his eternality by stating his oneness with the Father and his existence before Abraham. And these claims were met with fierce resistance as the religious leaders attempted to kill him during the Feast of

Tabernacles (six months before his death) and the Feast of Dedication (three months before his death). All the while, the gospel went out, people were changed, and the movement swelled.

Phase: Multiply
Phrase: "Come after me and bear fruit."
Verses: Luke 9:23; John 15:8
Time: Nine months

12 KEY EVENTS DURING THE MULTIPLY PHASE OF JESUS' MINISTRY

1. *Caesarea Philippi (Matt. 16:13–20; Mark 8:27–30; Luke 9:18–21)*
2. Jesus' first prediction of his death (Matt. 16:21–26; Mark 8:31–37; Luke 9:22–25)
3. *Transfiguration (Matt. 17:1–8; Mark 9:2–8; Luke 9:28–36)*
4. Jesus' second prediction of his death (Matt. 17:22–23; Mark 9:30–32; Luke 9:43–44)
5. *Feast of Tabernacles and attempt to kill Jesus (John 7:11–10:21)*
6. *Sent the Seventy-Two (Luke 10:1–16)*
7. Jesus warned his disciples (Luke 11:14–12:59)
8. *Feast of Dedication and attempt to kill Jesus (John 10:22–39)*
9. The cost of discipleship (Luke 14:25–35)
10. *Raised Lazarus (John 11:17–44)*
11. Jesus' third prediction of his death (Luke 18:31–34)
12. Salvation of Zacchaeus (Luke 19:1–10)

**Italics indicate the events that are included in the top thirty events of the life of Jesus*

NOTES

1. "Several Dead After Amtrack Train Traveling at 80 Mph Derails from Bridge onto I-5," *Seattle Times*, December 18, 2017, seattletimes.com/seattle-news/train-derails-from-bridge-onto-interstate-5-near-olympia/.

2. "Amtrack Didn't Wait for System That Could've Prevented Wreck," CBS News, December 20, 2017, dfw.cbslocal.com/2017/12/20/amtrak-system-prevented-derailment/.

3. T. J. Thinakaran, "The Genius with 1,000 Helpers," Open View, June 23, 2021, openviewpartners.com/blog/genius-with-1000-helpers/#.YdjGci1h3q1.

4. "From High School to Pro—How Wany Will Go?" Georgia State University, 2006, whenyoucantgopro.weebly.com/uploads/2/6/5/2/26529572/from_high_school_to_pro_statistics.pdf.

5. Charita Goshay, "'Difficult Days Are Ahead' for America's Churches, Faith Institutions," *Akron Beacon Journal*, August 22, 2020, beaconjournal.com/story/news/local/2020/08/22/lsquodifficult-days-are-aheadrsquo-for-americarsquos-churches-faith-institutions/42282593/.

6. Aaron Earls, "Mega Churches Continue to (Mostly) Grow and Not Just in Size," Lifeway Research, December 15, 2020, lifewayresearch.com/2020/12/15/megachurches-continue-to-mostly-grow-and-not-just-in-size/.

7. Rod Dreher, *Live Not by Lies* (New York: Sentinel, 2020), 5.

8. Ray Vander Laan, That the World May Know, Zondervan, thattheworldmayknow.com/define-talmid.

9. Lois Tverberg, "Covered in the Dust of Your Rabbi: An Urban Legend?" Our Rabbi Jesus, January 27, 2012, ourrabbijesus.com/covered-in-the-dust-of-your-rabbi-an-urban-legend/.

10. *Thayer's Greek Lexicon*, s.v. *"akoloutheo,"* accessed February 1, 2022, biblehub.com/greek/190.htm.

11. C. S. Lewis, *Mere Christianity* (New York: HarperOne, 2015), 199–200.

12. Ignatius of Antioch: Earliest Post-New Testament Martyr, *Christianity Today*, christianitytoday.com/history/people/martyrs/ignatius-of-antioch.html.

13. Michel J. Wilkins, *Following the Master* (Grand Rapids: Zondervan, 1992), 317.

14. Ibid., 324.

15. Ibid., 327.

16. Robert Thomas and Stanley Gundry, *The NIV Harmony of the Gospels* (San Francisco: HarperCollins, 1988).

17. Lindy Lowry, "The Growing Witness in Iran: Pastor Wahid's Story," Nations, March 4, 2020, nationsmedia.org/pastor-wahids-story/.

18. David Mathis, "If Billy Graham Had Been a Pastor," Desiring God, August 4, 2010, desiringgod.org/articles/if-billy-graham-had-been-a-pastor.

19. George Hunder, *The Celtic Way of Evangelism* (Nashville: Abingdon Press, 2010), 2.

20. Ibid., 13.

21. I would like to acknowledge the thoughtful contribution of Mac Lake and Brian Beauford on this subject. Their training videos have been instrumental to my thinking.

22. William Shakespeare, *The Tempest* in *The Complete Works of Shakespeare*, ed. David Bevington, 5th ed. (New York: Pearson, 2004), 1586.

23. Josh Buice, "Luther and Discipleship," Delivered by Grace, September 29, 2017, g3min.org/luther-and-discipleship/.

24. Carissa Jones, "Martin Luther's 'Table Talks' in Relation to His Theology of Discipleship," January 15, 2020, historicaltheology.org/articles/2020/1/11/martin-luthers-table-talks-in-relation-to-his-theology-of-discipleship.

25. "Luther's Small Catechism," Luther's Preface, 2019, catechism.cph.org.

26. John Calvin, *Institutes of the Christian Religion*, ed. John T. McNeill, trans. Ford Lewis Battles (Philadelphia: Westminster, 1960), 2:1460–61 (4.19.13).

27. Basil Miller, *John Wesley* (Bloomington, MN: Bethany House Publishers, 1973), 86.

28. Mark A. Maddix, "John Wesley's Small Groups: Models of Christian Community," *Holiness Today*, November/December 2009, holinesstoday.org/imported-news/john-wesleys-small-groups-models-christian-community.

29. Jason Byassee, "Methodists and Microcredit," *First Things*, November 2009, firstthings.com/article/2009/11/methodists-microcredit.

30. Eric Metaxas, *Seven Men* (Nashville: Thomas Nelson, 2013), 99.

31. Dietrich Bonhoeffer, *The Cost of Discipleship* (London: SCM, 1959), 99.

32. Charles R. Swindoll, *Intimacy with the Almighty* (Dallas: Word Publishing, 1996),10–11.

33. Michael Richardson, *Amazing Faith* (Colorado Springs: WaterBrook Press, 2000), 53.

34. "Bill Bright Memorial," CRU, cru.org/us/en/about/billbright/profile.html.

35. Richard Sisk, "Gates Wanted McChrystal to Fight for His Job," Military.com, February 3, 2014, military.com/daily-news/2014/02/03/gates-wanted-mcchrystal-to-fight-for-his-job.html.

36. Ram Charan, Steve Drotter, and Jim Noel, *The Leadership Pipeline* (San Francisco: Jossey-Bass Press), 63–64.

37. Angela Duckworh, *Grit: The Power of Passion and Perseverance* (New York: Scribner Book Company, 2016), quoted in Jenni Stahlmann

and Jody Hagaman, "Parenting: Grit Is a Determining Factor for Success," *Herald-Tribune*, March 25, 2019, heraldtribune.com/story/news/local/manatee/2019/03/25/parenting-grit-is-determining-factor-for-success/5628253007/.

38. R. Albert Mohler Jr., "Are You Called?" The Southern Baptist Theological Seminary, sbts.edu/are-you-called/.

39. Bonhoeffer, 99.

40. Ken Blanchard and Phil Hodges, *Lead Like Jesus* (Nashville: Thomas Nelson, 2008), 40.

41. David Garrison, *A Wind in the House of Islam* (Monument, CO: Wigtake, 2014), 5.

42. Ibid., 18.

43. Ibid., 123, 130–133.

44. Questions are adapted from *The Leadership Pipeline*, 123–124.

45. "Burkina Faso Attack: At Least 160 Killed in Village Raid," BBC News, June 6, 2021, bbc.com/news/world-africa-57368536.

46. Robert E. Coleman, *The Master Plan of Evangelism* (Grand Rapids: Revell, 1963), 107.

47. Robert Thomas and Stanley Gundry, 7.

ABOUT THE AUTHOR

CRAIG ETHEREDGE is an author and local church pastor. He holds a master of divinity from Southwestern Baptist Theological Seminary and a doctor of ministry from Trinity Evangelical Divinity School. He is the president and founder of discipleFIRST Ministries, which trains pastors and leaders nationally and internationally. He was a contributing author to Lifeway's *Disciple's Path* project and is the cofounder of the CrossCreek Network, which plants disciple-making churches all over the world. Etheredge also teaches discipleship courses as an adjunct professor at Southwestern Baptist Theological Seminary. He lives with his wife, Liz, in the Dallas-Fort Worth area, where he pastors a local church and invests his life in the next generation of leaders.